AI PRIMER FOR BUSINESS LEADERS

— ◉ ◯ ◉ —

Demystifying Generative AI

James Rowe

james@roweinnovations.com

AI Primer for Business Leaders
Demystifying Generative AI
by James Rowe
Copyright © 2024 Rowe Innovations, LLC
Published by SkillBites LLC
www.skillbites.net

DISCLAIMER AND/OR LEGAL NOTICES

Internet addresses given in this book were accurate at the time it went to press.

First Edition

Printed in the United States of America

For more information or to place bulk orders, contact the author or the publisher at info@skillbites.net

Cover image by rawpixel.com - Freepik.com

ISBN: 979-8-9912176-1-3 eBook
ISBN: 979-8-9912176-0-6 paperback

Dedicated to my children: Ethan, Audrey, Gracie, Maddie.

May they thrive in this future.

Personal Disclaimer

https://roweinnovations.com/
james@roweinnovations.com

Table of Contents

Introduction

It seems that you can't go far without seeing something in the news about OpenAI's ChatGPT product and the advances of generative AI technologies. This powerful new tool is hailed as both the next big innovative technology that will usher in huge productivity improvements and the harbinger of job destruction.[1] The truth will fall somewhere in between. For now, leaders at every level should be studying how generative AI works and its limitations in order to ensure that they and their companies have the greatest chances of success capitalizing on this technology's rapidly expanding capabilities.

With ChatGPT and DALEE-E, OpenAI has proven the commercial viability of user-friendly products that can surface mostly accurate information from extremely large datasets. These generative artificial intelligence (AI) services based on advancements leveraging large language models (LLMs) have demonstrated real-world productivity improvements across workers of all skill levels, but especially for those doing cognitive-based knowledge work previously thought immune from robotic automation.

However, we are still very early in the exploration of AI innovation and its applications to business;[2] you need look no further than very public corporate blunders[3] for proof of this. Corporate adoption of AI will have to navigate the evolving legislation and pending litigation pertaining to copyright law, fair use, and data privacy. Regardless of the status quo, it's important for business leaders at all levels to understand the current landscape of these tools, identifying their potential benefits and pitfalls to learn how best to leverage them.

Within this primer, I provide context and observations on an innovation as transformational as ERP systems and cloud native web applications: a new method of data search that harnesses the power of the past half-century of digitized human knowledge; a method of search that is able to identify and detect patterns previously only perceptible, if at all, to the most advanced disciples of that profession. This seemingly overnight breakthrough sensation is ten years in the making and can be traced to Google's DeepMind infamous "Move 37"[4] made while playing the strategy game go. Generative AI continues a trajectory that is bound to improve in the coming years, and effectively leveraging this new innovation warrants critical thought.

OpenAI and ChatGPT Takes a First Mover Market Advantage

You'd be forgiven for thinking that OpenAI and ChatGPT[i] were the only two providers of AI products,[5] especially because since 2019, OpenAI has been at the forefront[6] of releasing new models[ii] with a

---

i. In 2023, 57 percent of survey respondents had heard of ChatGPT—the highest of all identified models. Jacob Kastrenakes and James Vincent, "Hope, Fear, and AI," *The Verge*, June 26, 2023, https://www.theverge.com/c/23753704/ai-chatgpt-data-survey-research/.

ii. This was my first signal that ChatGPT was gaining awareness in the engineering community: https://news.slashdot.org/story/22/12/04/0248249/what-is-chatgpt-the-ai-chatbot-thats-taking-the-internet-by-storm/.

particular focus on having an accessible user interface.[iii] While it is an oversimplification to refer to all LLM generative products as "AI," many of the current AI services[iv] are based on a series of steps: data aggregation, building neural nets, and using predictive statistical models to provide seemingly "magical" outputs, i.e., generative AI.[v]

Until OpenAI launched ChatGPT, there wasn't an easy-to-use, consumer-focused generative AI product on the market, and the way this product was released to the public is innovative in its own regard. OpenAI's deliberate product decision to render ChatGPT's responses letter by letter gives it that "generative" feel instead of hiding the completed response behind a loading bar and grants a sensation of watching the machine "at work" and provides that "wow" factor, launching the service into the news cycle. The focused minimal design and eschewing of ads at launch meant that users could focus on getting answers to their queries—something that has felt broken[7] in traditional search engines for a few years now.

OpenAI has continuously improved ChatGPT and was the preferred model announced during the "Apple Intelligence"[8] portion of Apple's 2024 developer keynote. ChatGPT is also a selectable model with Microsoft 365 Copilot. Both companies have announced that more generative AI models will be available in the future, but for now, ChatGPT seems synonymous with AI.

---

iii. Specifically referring to https://chatgpt.com, its left column search history, central call to action "Message ChatGTP," and the drop-down to select a model to work with.

iv. These include but are not limited to ChatGPT, Bard, Gemini, Perplexity, Meta AI (Llama), Microsoft Copilot, Github Copilot, and various other vendor-specific products marketed as AI.

v. I'm primally focused here on text systems, not audio or visual systems.

Since OpenAI launched ChatGPT, seemingly every tech company has announced some form of AI integration. Microsoft and GitHub launched Copilot,[9] Alphabet introduced Bard alongside some of its search results,[10] and Meta has deployed Meta AI, built with Llama 3, into its Facebook product.[11] All of these integrations have been rushed into service on the heels of ChatGPT's earlier releases, none reaching the level of coverage that ChatGPT has enjoyed in the media.

The AI industry is rapidly changing, and we are still very early both on the technology adoption bell curve and the Gartner Hype Cycle.[12] Even if you count every company that has released some new AI product, they are a small percentage of the overall S&P 500 and even smaller subset of the broader total stock market. Instead of looking at companies that have released a generative AI product, what's more useful is looking at corporate adoption of generative AI. A McKinsey & Company survey from early 2024 found that 65 percent of organizations are regularly using generative AI within their business.[13]

As for employees of those companies, regardless of the specific product used, knowledge workers appear to be leading the adoption of generative AI services, with a 2023 survey on fishbowl.com finding that "43% of professionals have used AI tools, including ChatGPT, for work-related tasks. Nearly 70% of those professionals are doing so without their boss's knowledge."[14] The adoption has only increased since this survey was taken, and the lack of transparency from workers seems driven by a lack of official company policies and the perception of automating their own work. Further opaque terms and conditions pertaining to data retention and using consumer queries to train future models has businesses concerned about protecting their intellectual property.[15]

According to a more recent study by Microsoft in June of 2024, "79 percent of knowledge workers said they had started using AI in their job."[16] Regardless of the exact percentage, it's clear that employees at all levels are finding and leveraging these tools with or without their companies' knowledge. Lest you think this is a fad you can ignore like NFTs or blockchain, there are already early victims of the adoption of ChatGPT and other generative AI tools.

The ability to quickly generate code solutions with generative AI has reduced site visits to stackoverflow.com (a common reference site for software engineers) 6 percent monthly since January 2022.[17] The company's response is also worth evaluating as it seems to be struggling to navigate this new future. First stackoverflow.com restricted the posting of AI-generated answers, releasing a policy that AI-generated answers are not allowed,[18] and now they've launched their own generative AI tool called "Overflow AI."[19] Another business casualty is Chegg, a one-to-one tutoring and writing help service that matches students with a live person to help them through assignments. Since the advent of ChatGPT, investors seem to think Chegg's target customer will use a free generative AI product instead of a live employee. A report from May 2023 shows their stock has plummeted over 40 percent.[20]

While it's too early to predict the future of every company, every single one will have to access its own offerings and how best to navigate this new innovation. As detailed in future chapters, there is a spectrum of disruption depending on how much automatable repeated cognitive work is performed in any given role. Understanding the business model of your own company and how it will be impacted by generative AI will be the first task at hand for business leaders.

Demystifying Generative AI

A look under the hood of generative AI services reveals a common build process tracing to a paper written by engineers[21] working at Google that added a new concept called "transforms" to existing data analysis processes. Mathematicians[vi] will be right at home with the inner workings of generative AI as the generative output is based on the statistical matching of word sequence based on the context set by the user query and an enormously large training data set.

Stephen Wolfram has a most excellent deep dive into what ChatGPT is doing and how it works,[22] but for our purposes, the ghost inside the machine of all large language model (LLM) generative AI services is a combination of large datasets, training methodologies, and system configuration that influences the outputs of said service. At the shallowest level, in addition to the source datasets, the system configuration consists of model temperature, top-p, and top-k.[23] These are critical to understanding all generative AI products; it should be noted that currently, ChatGPT and other public AI services do not allow for user configuration of these settings:

James: "Can I set your temperature, top-p or top-k directly?"

Chat-GPT4o: "No, you can't set parameters like temperature, top-p, or top-k directly in this interface."

Once a user provides a prompt, it is parsed using these system configurations, then generative AI makes mathematically guided guesses on what sequence of words best matches the prompt based on its analy-

---

vi. https://xkcd.com/435/. Purity.

sis of datasets it was trained on.[vii] This "training dataset" is a vast repository of digital content, either private or public; it should be noted that the collection of said public copyrighted data by private for-profit corporations is currently under scrutiny. To date, ChatGPT product demos thus far have focused on the ability to respond to a generic high-level request and produce a coherent response that is both useful and appears "magical."[viii]

While it may appear magical, this is a concept already in everyday consumer products, albeit on a tiny scale. Autocorrect, predictive text,[24] and early chatbots all use very specific contexts and finite scenarios to connect user intent with close-enough correct outcomes. These simple mechanisms are primarily based on keyword identification and can only work with a few tokens or perhaps one sentence at a time. Generative AI scales these concepts and produces a response with hundreds and soon thousands of words. A useful analogy to this process is to think about a hypothetical librarian who has read every single word in the training dataset provided (the library) and is able to provide an "answer" to a user prompt based on pattern matching from all of the data provided to them. It's crucial to understand that generative AI does not "know" the answer; it merely attempts to match the prompt to corresponding text in its dataset.

---

vii. Again, I'm focusing on written text, not audio and visual. Who is to say that an auto AI-generated transcript of a YouTube video is a high-quality original work? Or, least of all, a YouTube video with auto-generated captions in a second language transcribed and incorporated into a training model?

viii. I reiterate here that I think one of the brilliant aspects of ChatGPT was the conscious decision to "show" the text output as a data stream instead of a "result." Had they chosen to put up a spinning loading bar and just return text, I don't think it would have had the same impact as watching ChatGPT "at work."

Generative AI products take this system of "when the user requests X, a valuable response is Y" and scale it to the extreme of all data contained within its training dataset. Revisiting the aforementioned system configuration parameters, we can see how they directly influence the generated output. Temperature, top-p, and top-k all control how "random" or "measured" a response is. These are currently some of the most well-known configuration attributes; there are more, and even when two users provide the same prompt, they might get two different answers based on the combination of factors that contribute to a generative AI system. This contrasts to traditional search results where generally the same search queries from multiple users return similar if not identical results.

For example, in the English sentence, "Have a _____," what might come next? "Good day"? "Slice of pizza"? With this very simplistic approach, a generative AI model configured with low values of temperature, top-p, and top-k would answer with a very predictable "good day" in its best customer service voice every time, whereas a generative AI model configured with high system parameters might answer, "Have a stupendous day you amazing person."[ix] Going back to our librarian analogy, these system configurations control how predictable and useful said librarian is—almost its temperament. Configured with too much entropy (high values), the generated response might be scattered or not even make cognitive sense; with too little entropy (low values), every response will be bland and lifeless or not take full advantage of the training data. I will let ChatGPT have the final say on its configuration referring to my prompt to set system configuration directly.

---

ix. Even I didn't know what was coming next.

James: "How would you describe those parameters as it relates to your outputs?"

ChatGPT-4o: "In summary, lower values for these parameters make the output more focused and predictable, while higher values make it more diverse and creative."

30k-Foot View of the Generative AI Lifecycle

Let's pull together all these concepts—datasets, training methodology, system configuration, user queries, and generative results—into a high level thirty-thousand-foot context diagram. Because we are focused on demystifying generative AI concepts, this diagram summarizes some more advanced parts of building a generative AI product to maintain this high-level overview.

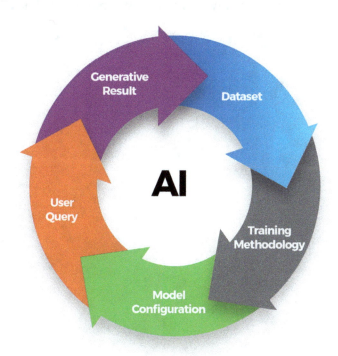

Start at the top and enter on arrow "Dataset": a generative AI model is only as good as the data that serves as the foundation for all future steps. The dataset process will include sourcing and preparing it for the training methodology. When companies refer to the "algorithm" of generative AI, they are almost always referring to the training methodology, which includes practices such as adversarial networks or autoregressive modeling. The specific methodologies will change as the field advances, but combining datasets with a training methodology prepares the system for model configuration. As covered, this will include the cost considerations of system architecture, parameter tuning, and model validation: everything that is needed to prepare a solution that is capable of returning responses to user queries (prompts). Once a system is generating outputs, it is inevitable that these published outputs will be included in future datasets either intentionally as a feedback mechanism or inadvertently through consumption of public data.

The Bedrock of Generative AI: High Quality Data

The importance of high-quality source datasets cannot be understated. The utility of any generative AI solution will be built upon the source data acquired. Currently, datasets are sourced from anywhere and everywhere possible.[x] As generative AI products are released and benchmarked,[xi] they often indicate a "dataset size"[25] that can be thought of as the amount of source data used to make all future educated guesses in response to customer queries.

The totality[xii] of data available to train on is thought to be finite, or at the very least, yielding diminishing returns over time. Further,

---

x. Enter copyright law. Creating a training set of millions of examples almost always requires first copying many more millions of images, videos, audio, or text-based works. Mark A. Lemley and Bryan Casey, "Fair Learning," *Texas Law Review* 99 (2021): 743-785.

xi. All models reference their score on some benchmark or another, but it's my opinion that we don't have a good benchmark concept for measuring the raw capabilities of a model. This will come later. https://www.nature.com/articles/d41586-024-01087-4.

xii. We estimate the stock of human-generated public text at around 300 trillion tokens. If trends continue, language models will fully employ this stock between 2026 and 2032, or even earlier if intensely overtrained. Pablo Villalobos et al., "Will We Run Out of Data? Limits of LLM Scaling Based on Human-Generated Data," *Epoch AI*, June 6, 2024, https://epochai.org/blog/will-we-run-out-of-data-limits-of-llm-scaling-based-on-human-generated-data/.

with the explosion of generative AI products, many public sources of data are updating their terms and conditions to protect their data from robotic scraping; other datasets are moving behind paywalls or being taken down altogether. This is one of the most rapidly changing areas of AI, and I predict private companies will need to leverage their internal private data to be competitive with their AI solutions.

The value of this human-created data is reflected in the large deals[26] signed for exclusive rights to use it for training. Having access to high-quality datasets is a competitive advantage that increases the value of any individual generative AI product. Complementing the generative AI lifecycle diagram, the available data for training can be thought of as a series of concentric circles that are rapidly expanding and contracting based on government legislation, litigation, and changes in terms of service by companies,[27] with "All Data of All Time" being the upper bounds of available data and "Public Domain Data" being the smallest set of known data that is free to use in a commercial product.

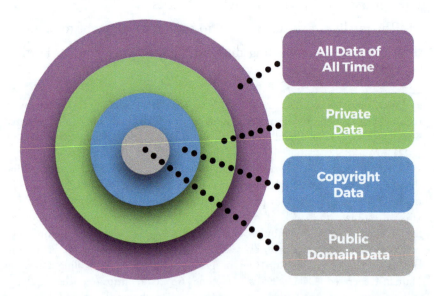

Finding a way to catalogue and comprehend the totality of human published works has always been a distinctly human project, whether through a formal encyclopedia publication, the Google Books project, or crowdsourced via Wikipedia. A big promise of generative AI solutions is providing a way to surface relevant information from these vast data repositories in response to user queries—with the caveat that responses are an output reflective of predictions based on training data, not an authoritative one based on wisdom. I cover some examples of this in the "Personal Use of ChatGPT" Appendix and how it's especially true as it pertains to "smushing" different source materials into one output.

To illustrate the importance of dataset selection, let's revisit our librarian metaphor and presume the training dataset only contains American dessert recipe books published during the 1950s and 60s. Gelatin and Jell-O creations may dominate in this era, but would not hold up across the context of all recipes in history. If one set of material is overrepresented in training data—or worse, missing altogether—that will be reflected in the predictive outputs and limit the utility of the response or, worse, reflect the biases of the very human decision about which data to include.

Suddenly, the prompt "What desserts would you recommend making at home" returns Jell-O salad instead of chocolate chip cookies. This same concept applies to human biases and prejudices—a generative AI product is only as good as the training data it's based on. If history belongs to the victors, then what of the fragmented perspectives of the losers? If they aren't digitally represented in the training dataset, generative AI will be unable to provide any outputs referencing them.

Critical Thought: Dataset Limitations

Let's revisit our librarian again to understand the limitations of readily available public data used for training in today's generative AI products. With so much of the publicly available data coming from Anglo-Western society, current generative AI results skew toward that context. For example, in 2014, Amazon stopped work on an algorithmic approach to evaluating resumes for hiring as the underlying dataset was over-representative of white men with computer science degrees.[28] Another documented bias in training data is prompting OpenAI's DALL-E to create an image of a successful businessperson, to which it will likely return a Western perception of success: older white men in business suits.[29]

Unlike a library that has a catalogue of materials, currently, there is no way to directly inspect the training dataset used by generative AI models, which are often cited as a competitive advantage or a trade secret. Researchers have been able to successfully use generative AI products to reproduce known copyrighted material, leading to the suspicion it is contained in the training datasets. There have been requests that companies make public both the underlying datasets and the training methodologies to ensure compliance with all laws and regulations. This will be critical to understanding any implications for new generative AI services built and brought to market.

In addition to not knowing what's in the "library" of training data, generative AI products seem to struggle with sarcasm, satire, and contextual clues that keep them from distinguishing helpful fact from sarcastic answer. To be fair, humans fail at this as well—for example, sharing articles from *The Onion* as fact. A recent example cited in various news articles was a generative search result that adding glue to a cheese pizza makes it "stick better," and eating rocks can improve your health.[30] Aside from being unhelpful and potentially dangerous, it seems the generative AI "predicted" these as solutions based on specific Reddit posts likely present in its training dataset.

There is another danger to generative AI results: the Mandela effect,[31] where the collective shared memory of a group supersedes the actual reality of the situation. In the aforementioned example, if enough people publish online content with incorrect information, generative AI will likely see this as correct. In the early days of web search, "Google bombing"[32] was the attempt to mislead search results by associating keywords with specific websites or images; the future might contain "AI bombing," where large datasets are sold seeded with misinformation in an attempt to influence outputs. A critical inspection of the data used for training is crucial for generating useful and correct generative outputs.

Finally, with generative AI tools becoming readily available for everyone a new slang term has popped up for AI generated content online: "slop."[33] It's not quite spam, and it's not human, but it exists. The creation of this content is poisoning the well of knowledge on Google Books[34] and shutting down scientific journals overwhelmed by AI-generated submissions.[35] Real human contributors are shut out as they try to compete with low-quality AI-generated content, and at the forefront of this adoption (from the consumer perspective) are spam websites trying to boost their search rank scores and grab ad dollars.[36]

It's important to identify the presence of AI-generated content in your own training datasets, as recursive training on AI generated content will eventually lead to model collapse.[37] Some have suggested ending training datasets at 2021; this will quickly be outpaced by human discovery, and, because text generated by AI models is statistically correct, attempts at detecting it have so far eluded automation. At some point in the future, the majority of digital content will be produced by generative AI. When most readily available public data is AI-generated, knowing which data will make the most effective generative AI products will be a new role humanity needs to fill.

The Umbrella of "Fair Use" and Generative AI

There are a number of pending legal cases[38] and ethical issues that need resolution pertaining to the inputs and outputs of generative AI that anyone should consider as they adopt generative AI solutions in their products, services, and work. Even though AI companies aren't currently making training data public, it is presumed that the datasets are based on the digitization of a huge swath of humanity's published works.[xiii] These digital works range from being in the public domain to having strong copyrights with requirements for written permission from the copyright holder to use any portion thereof. Because generative AI companies are using robotic scraping and purchasing digital data to fuel their datasets, there is a clash between copyright holders and service providers. Historically, there has been deference to the use of robotic digital copying of material by companies, but the citing of "fair use" by OpenAI and others is currently under scrutiny.

Again, because it's presumed that companies like OpenAI have scraped much of the publicly available web, they have been sued for copyright infringement by multiple trade groups. OpenAI has indicated in court filings[39] that because its outputs are transformative of the

---

xiii. "The public web has at least several billion human-written pages, with altogether perhaps a trillion words of text ..., more than 5 million digitized books have been made available (out of 100 million or so that have ever been published), giving another 100 billion or so words of text." Wolfram, "What Is ChatGPT Doing."

inputs, this qualifies as fair use.[xiv] However, the company has provided no mechanism by which copyright holders can opt out, identify their data in training sets, or even attempt to build a product using only data known to belong to the public domain.

OpenAI has also said that "limiting training data to public domain books and drawings created more than a century ago might yield an interesting experiment, but would not provide AI systems that meet the needs of today's citizens."[40] Independent researchers have been able to use prompts to regenerate entire copyrighted works,[41] calling into question whether OpenAI and others have respected existing copyright law by taking copyright content and incorporating it into their commercial product.

A few big tech firms have formed a lobbying group that seeks to educate legislators and consumers on the topic—in their favor, of course.[42] In this material, they cite that one of the uses of programmatic "reading" is to provide insights and further advancement to the humans using that material. Thus far, courts have taken a permissive view of this learning model of copying, but it remains to be seen if that continues with these recent innovations in the generative AI field.

Harvard Business Review has a good summary[43] of what the courts are being asked to define, such as their interpretations of what constitutes a "derivative work" and the "transformative use of copyright material." One way to circumvent all of these challenges is to only include data in the training sets that has known copyright heritage or to work with a generative AI service provider that agrees to take on the liability of any copyright infringement.

---

xiv. Given the doctrinal uncertainty and the rapid development of ML technology, it is unclear whether machine copying will continue to be treated as fair use. Lemley and Casey, "Fair Learning."

Copyright Holders and Compensation

Two themes have emerged from the various court cases currently navigating through the justice system. First is that corporations can identify and recognize[44] that copyright holders can be negotiated with and compensated for their works, as we've seen previously with the compensation model change for actors, the transition from syndication to streaming of movies and television shows, and the streaming compensation in the music industry.[45] Second is that the invention of a new transformation process does not negate or strip the rights of copyright holders to license that work for capital gain.

As it pertains to fair use, courts will need to decide if a for-profit company can programmatically copy all digital content and repackage it as a paid product irrespective of a copyright holder's rights. Without legislative change or court rulings, it seems unlikely that corporations will provide a way for copyright holders to search datasets and prove that their content is being used and thus in need of citation/compensation. Many of these cases will need to be argued and settled to identify a new compensation model for copyright holders and to address the ethics of appropriate fair use.[46]

Additionally, it seems awfully convenient that many of the first generative AI companies that have vacuumed up all of this public data[47] are now calling for regulations and data protections after they've already acquired their commanding lead. How might a new company compete when all new data acquisition is met with large costs and purchase agreements? They key takeaway here is that source datasets may become a source of liability, and the surest way to avoid it is to only include data with clearly negotiated copyright license agreements.

AI Impact on Businesses

As of July 2024, 96 percent[48] of organizations now report discussing generative AI in the boardroom. This discussion also has spread to earnings calls with over 90 percent[49] of technology companies in the S&P 500 referring to AI. The push to embed AI experiences in products has only intensified with many companies rushing new solutions to market. Technology has always been an accelerator for business productivity, and generative AI is no different. The question is: How will businesses integrate these new capabilities into their companies?

Let's first compare generative AI to past technological innovations. Generative AI is not the second coming of the internet or even a universal disrupter across industries as was the adoption of computers in the workforce. It is not as disruptive as the steam engine or other industrial innovations. I would argue that generative AI has the same productivity leveraging capabilities as an ERP/CRM adoption, the availability of location data via GPS, or the productivity increases gained by shared knowledge systems like collaborative document editing systems and other digital collaboration tools.

Generative AI integration into business will both improve the productivity of existing workers and lower the cost of doing business. The last major technology revolution that generative AI currently echoes is the commercialization of GPS. Consider the evolution of GPS from military use only, to commercial availability, then to dedicated stand-alone products, and finally onto our phones enabling an entire ecosystem of location-aware apps. Generative AI is a foundational tool that will need to be fitted to specific processes and workflows that it can enhance to benefit company adoption along this same path. Broadly, there hasn't been a time in history when a new technology has resulted in fewer jobs for people.[50] There are disruptions, and, at an individual level, there are winners and losers. But to say that AI will result in mass unemployment feels hyperbolic.

Over the past 10-plus years there have already been very context-specific generative AI automations; for example, sports reporting has adopted generative AI to produce recaps of minor league baseball games since 2016. This same approach is also used in the analysis of earnings calls.[51] Neither of these advancements mean there are fewer sports writers or stock analysts. Look no further than your favorite online forum or nontraditional broadcasting source for the expansion of humans in these domains.

Early studies have found that generative AI has the potential to automate or augment up to 100 percent of various knowledge work processes.[52] These automatable functions of a job usually pertain to gathering information, applying it to a work in progress, making a decision, and/or informing the customer. Generative AI has the potential to greatly improve the productivity of existing knowledge workers, as reviewed in some initial case studies below.

Improve Employee Onboarding and Training

Today's generative AI maturity lends itself to experimentation and iteration on internal training tools that can be directly observed. Especially with case law pending on copyright and fair use, rushing a product to external-facing customers can have disastrous consequences for your goodwill and company brand, and it can potentially expose you to liability in regulated industries.

Companies typically understand that it can take up to 12 months of experience and training in the role before a new hire becomes fully productive.[53] Below is a hypothetical plot of an experience curve comparing an employee with traditional training and one augmented by a generative AI agent or service. Early studies have indicated that nearly all workers experience productivity improvements when leveraging AI tools, and those starting with the least experience have benefited the most. Having a generative AI product that can help onboard employees will decrease the expense of training and accelerate their time to peak productivity.

Look at the following graph, which is hypothetical but reflects data charts in the cited works. The green line represents an employee who might be hired and spend several months learning their role either through formal training programs, on the job training, or self-paced learning management systems. Their respective productivity would inflect at respective knowledge "aha" moments along the way until they reached some level of peak productivity in the tasks of that role. Contrast that with an employee paired with either a generic generative AI tool like ChatGPT or a specifically trained one with privately sourced data (the dotted blue line). The employees start at the same point, but a paired AI agent can rapidly onboard new employees, is always available, and helps the employee reach a higher peak productivity than can be reached by an employee without an augmented workflow. JPMorgan Chase has just recently released for internal use a generative AI toolset that will provide productivity improvements in their finance departments.[54] Their new and existing employees will now be capable of operating on this higher frontier with the knowledge of a privately trained generative AI product.

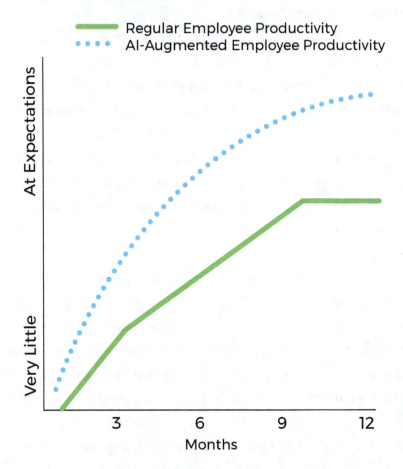

Reduce Operating Expenses

Generative AI products have also established proof of decreasing operating expenses for businesses of every size. Suppose your company needs to respond to a regulatory change that impacts the services you offer to your customers. Someone (or many someones) has to be constantly reading legislation, be aware of the change, analyze what it means to the business, decide if action is needed, and write a brief to share that decision with impacted departments. Then, in the context of software, a project scope is written, requirements are developed, and the software is built, tested, and released. Then more memos are written and training guides are developed. All of this before the change to company process ever generates revenue for the business.

Each of these touchpoints incurs an operational expense to the company. If there were an ideal path from external stimulus to process change, it would involve the least amount of employee interaction to improve said good or service. Early generative AI products have been deployed in call centers with great effect on operational expense,[55] as detailed below. In addition to capturing inbound customer queries, the potential power of generative AI is to act as an autonomous agent supplementing existing company employees.

Think back to the librarian and the library. Consider a world in which every employee has available to them a librarian versed in the materials belonging to the company. Currently referred to as "AI agents," I think they are one of the biggest opportunities for business to combine the collective institutional knowledge of employees with internal datasets. These AI agents would provide support and context to the business as it operates. This includes every function of the business, but those with repetitive digital cognitive tasks are best suited for either replacement or augmentation.[56] In the above example, a model trained on past training documents, requirements, and project definitions can greatly speed the business's response to new product requirements.

A word of caution: while these productivity improvements will benefit the company bottom line, the money saved in operational expenses by generative AI are inevitably applied to other value-added tasks or reinvested in the business.[57] Even though the use of generative AI will span the entire organization, including the CEO,[58] many of these advantages will either be competed away or have their own expenses associated with them. The key is recognizing that to continue to be competitive, adoption is a matter of how and when, not if.

Early Real-World Generative AI Results

One company that has made its generative AI investments very public is Klarna, a payments and shopping service that was having to grow its customer support group linearly with its corresponding growth on the business side. It has since released several press updates on its adoption of AI, the operational cost savings, and impacts on customer service. Highlights include a generative AI chatbot performing the work of ~700 agents and saving the company $40 million a year in operating expenses.[59]

Another CEO posted about cutting 90 percent of the company's customer service department in favor of generative AI solutions.[60] A published research article quoted Krithivasan, head of Indian IT giant Tata Consultancy Services (TCS), saying that there could be minimal need for call centers in as little as one year.[61] Gartner has also identified call centers and customer interactions as prime candidates for the use of generative AI.[62]

Caution is warranted; there are also negative brand press and court cases with the use of generative AI in chatbots. Air Canada had to honor the bad information given by a chatbot to a customer,[63] and on a more humorous note, one Chevy dealership chatbot offered a customer a brand new Chevrolet Tahoe for $1, no takebacks.[64] There have been multiple releases and pullbacks of AI trials. Target is about

24

to trial a worker and shopper AI companion, but it is being deployed as an assistant to the human workers in the store,[65] whereas IBM and McDonald's recently abandoned an attempt to use AI to ease drive-through ordering.[66] Adopting generative AI services requires a strong evaluation framework, ability to audit outputs, a stomach for mistakes, and the integrity for accountability.

It should be noted that businesses aren't the only ones adopting generative AI; the ability to rapidly generate content allows unscrupulous actors to flood your external systems with fraud attempts. There are already sites that are creating realistic ID photos,[67] and recently, a firm fell victim to a voice deepfake that cost the company tens of millions of dollars.[68] Fraud attempts have historically been limited by the expense to perform key actions, but generative AI drives that price to near zero, giving incentive to try infinite attempts at fraud with very compelling voice and text mimics.

Critical Thought: AI Accountability and Hallucinations

Who is accountable for the decisions and "answers" provided by a generative AI system, especially if it is automated without human intervention or review? One need look no further than the British Postal Scandal[69] to see how software can ruin lives. In that scandal, despite warnings from end-users that the software was providing incorrect financial information, hundreds of people were prosecuted and jailed over incorrect data.

Generative AI has the same risks as it is relied on for business functions. As it pertains to internal generative AI models, a governance group needs to provide guidelines to ensure that AI models don't accomplish their objectives by shortcutting the process in unethical or illegal ways. It's important for all business implementations to have clear legal compliance evaluation as it pertains to deploying generative AIs that are capable of providing incorrect information to the customer.

The most critical aspect of building and deploying AI is the awareness that all generative AI is based on statistical pattern matching—not producing knowledge—and therefore relies on the user to interpret fact from fiction. If every response included a disclaimer that "This is random text," I think people would view the results with more skepticism. In my use of ChatGPT, there have been instances where a response was provided with a citation that led to an empty page, or facts and figures presented as truth that upon closer inspection were completely hypothetical.

Here in New York, a lawyer was sanctioned for including fictitious court citations.[70] His defense included that it was subcontracted work, and across state lines, but also that he was unaware that ChatGPT could produce fictitious information. I don't think the small disclaimer does justice to the amount of trouble that anyone can get into by using the outputs from generative AI products.

Below is an example where I prompted ChatGPT for data on LLC titles, and it was happy to oblige. When I asked for a source, it confessed the chart generated was based on hypothetical data, which I feel should've been disclosed in its response. "Here's a hypothetical chart" would have been clearer than "this should give you a sense."

James: "Can you show me a distribution of title names for LLCs?"

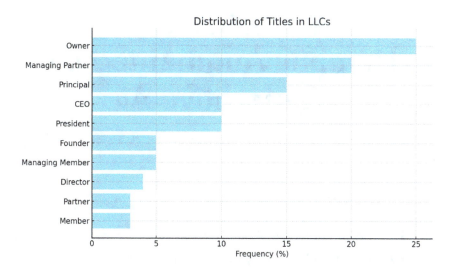

ChatGPT: "Here's a distribution of common titles used in LLCs, visualized in a bar chart. This should give you a sense of how frequently each title is used."

James: "Where did you get this data from?"

ChatGPT: "The data presented in the chart is a hypothetical distribution created for visualization purposes and is not sourced from actual statistics."

Humans Augmented by Generative AI

Harvard Business School published a working study on the use of ChatGPT with a variety of tasks, finding that some tasks were readily completable by AI while others remained outside its grasp. But the key point was that regardless of seniority, the people using generative AI tools got more done, more efficiently.[71]

Another working paper titled "Generative AI at Work"[72] found that AI augmentation helped customer service agents to close 14 percent more cases per hour; it helped lower-skilled employees the most. As reviewed, onboarding employees quickly while improving their productivity can cut training costs and improve the skillsets of new employees without taking time away from more experienced ones.

A generative AI model trained on the collection of a company's proprietary material would be able to augment and provide best-guess predictions to employee prompts far better than basic search of siloed data repositories. It has the potential to add depth to conversations not possible today, and with proper feedback loops, this AI agent would constantly be improving alongside the business. It could be a documentary specialist that can provide summaries of discussions and be queried with natural language. "What were the key points of yesterday's discussions?" "Who is waiting on me for a decision?" "What did we decide at that last meeting?" Currently, institutional knowledge is held by the longest-serving employees, whom we also rely on to provide situational awareness to new business projects. AI agents may soon provide a breadth of knowledge and history that transcends any one employee.

Employees can train on business processes and workflows in a hyper-contextual way without ever impacting end users or customers. This training set is refreshed and kept current with real customer data, making it evergreen for future models. Equipping employees with AI agents is the next evolution of autocorrect and predictive email completion. Don't stop at one: there are even experiments using two or three agents with different personas to mimic some of the collaboration of humans.[73] Building a virtual "team of rivals" can only enhance the value derived from these generative AI services.

The future power of generative AI lies in resolving a large proportion of automated tasks on behalf of the business independent of any human intervention. Think of the airline industry and the decades of improving autopilots for safer flight; generative AI in the workplace holds the same promise for cognitive tasks. In a world in which so many meetings and memos are to exchange status information, how many of them could be enhanced with the application of an AI agent?[74]

Generative AI can and will fail. The question is if it will fail at a rate tolerable to the business or relative to unassisted employees. To maintain integrity, it's important to maintain chain of custody on training datasets and have business continuity plans that accommodate failure. To complete our look at aviation, even in spite of all the advances with autopilots, human pilots are still expected to train for hundreds of hours. Flying a plane still requires hands-on experience to navigate exceptional circumstances.[75]

Building a Team of (AI Agent) Rivals

One of the more interesting things I've encountered while interacting with generative AI is "talking" out early ideas with ChatGPT as it pertains to decisions I make along the way in life. I would not recommend it for serious introspection, but who's to say future iterations won't be able to more fully grasp the outcomes of decision-making? An AI will never have to live with the emotional outcomes of your decisions, but it could make a parable that best relates to your own personal knowledge.

It's trivial to provide a concept to ChatGPT and then have it act out different roles as it inspects that idea. Here is an example as I contemplated switching from Google Workspace to Microsoft 365 for my personal use. Once I provided ChatGPT with some context of my current setup and the friction points and benefits I saw, I asked it to provide me with a list of stakeholders and what their concerns might be. I could easily see using an AI model to explore these concepts much as a SWOT analysis tool, MoSCoW analysis, or RACI methodologies are used today in evaluating business decisions.

> James: "Can you make a summary list of the stakeholders and concerns/benefits, limit two bullets per stakeholder group?"
>
> ChatGPT-4o:
>
> **Stakeholders, Concerns, and Benefits Summary**
>
> **End User (Excel Enthusiast)**
>
> **Concerns:** Learning new interface, Downtime during migration

Benefits: Advanced Excel features (Power Query, PivotTables, Macros/VBA), Better data visualization and integration with Power BI

End User (Google Workspace Expert)

Concerns: Learning curve for new tools, Initial disruption in productivity

Benefits: Access to robust Office apps and real-time co-authoring in Excel, Unified ecosystem with Microsoft apps and advanced security features

IT Manager/Administrator

Concerns: Ensuring data migration integrity and minimizing downtime, Providing adequate training and support

Benefits: Centralized administration and enhanced security and compliance, Better integration with Windows OS and robust admin tools

Project Managers/Team Leads

Concerns: Maintaining productivity during transition, Ensuring team collaboration tools are effective

Benefits: Enhanced project management tools (Teams, Planner), Streamlined communication and improved document management

Executives/Decision Makers

Concerns: Cost implications, Ensuring smooth transition without impacting business operations

Benefits: Access to advanced business tools and better security and compliance, Unified platform for all business operations

Software Engineering and Coding Help

Every other section in this book is based on research of cited materials, but because I have been a professional software engineer, I decided to take a deep dive into the advertised effectiveness of using generative AI with software engineering. This section is my own personal anecdotal experience, and I agree that AI is able to generate solutions given appropriate prompts. Currently, ChatGPT-4o has some shortcomings: it will waste compute cycles regenerating portions of code that are already working[xv] and cannot provide solutions within the context of a large system. The biggest challenge I see is that generative AI has no concept of the level of effort needed to execute and implement its suggestions. For example, one suggestion it provided to resolve my authorization (HTTP 403) errors was to switch hosting providers completely, which would be orders of magnitude more difficult than modifying permissions on my webserver.

ChatGPT seems to do very well at writing loop structures on data objects and generating mock data for unit testing, but I think the next iteration of AI will need more context awareness to be useful at designing and building full systems. GitHub has been advertising that Copilot makes engineers 56 percent more effective, but I think that overestimates the returns when making modifications to existing code with existing engineers. Again, there are also pending questions about the fair use of scanning online code.[76]

I estimate the actual productivity improvement to be in the 15-20 percent range. This is based on my personal use of ChatGPT-3.5 to write a Python script that parsed a CSV file and converted each row

---

xv. I've even experimented with generating patch files, which were not generated correctly for application.

to an individual Readme file.[77] Then when ChatGPT-4o was released, I used it to write a script that scrapped an old personal WordPress site and converted it to individual Readme files.[78] In both instances, ChatGPT was able to get me an initial working Python script fairly quickly. It also surprised me with "knowledge" about string formatting and makefiles—areas in which I did not have previous experience. But once it had accomplished roughly 60 percent of the task, I was back to the traditional software engineering tasks of coding and testing.

I included my ChatGPT chat history for both directly in their respective repositories. Could I have completed the tasks without ChatGPT? Likely, but with a lot more searching on Stack Overflow and cursing as I brute-forced various aspects of the script. I also wouldn't have included useful additions like a makefile or error handling. The best part of working with ChatGPT was being able to copy/paste error messages directly from my local console and have ChatGPT suggest context-aware solutions.

Some observations I have as a software engineer: ChatGPT would reinvent the wheel instead of using open-source libraries and has struggled to provide iterations to my code, especially with regex and data processing. The most frustrating part of the process was when ChatGPT would start to regenerate the entire piece of code I was working on instead of just generating an iteration. I think this would be mitigated by relying on in-IDE copilot.

One of the earliest examples that I can find online is the use of generative AI to automatically translate between two languages. DARPA is piloting a tool that can convert C code to Rust[79] but is having what I would consider rudimentary results. There still is the very manual process of an engineer taking an existing subroutine of code, copying it as a prompt to a generative AI tool, and then integrating the converted code back into the larger project. In the example of the C to Rust code, an engineer would still have to add tooling to support Rust, be able to troubleshoot it, and interact with both a C and Rust code base. This is not a trivial feat.

As I explore more in the "AI and Humanity" section, I had several existential crises as I saw ChatGPT generate what I always felt was the domain of a human being: working code. I tell myself we'll always have engineers because no human can describe a perfect system. But who's to say whether future software projects are just described outcomes with goals that AI will continuously rewrite black-box systems to accomplish? I'll let ChatGPT have the final word.

James: "What is my role as an engineer if anyone can come here and get the answer?"

ChatGPT-4o: "James, I get where you're coming from. It can feel frustrating when information that took years to master can be summarized so quickly … In essence, while quick answers are helpful, your expertise ensures those answers are implemented correctly, efficiently, and sustainably, which is something only someone with your experience can achieve."

Critical Thought: Prompt Injection and Generative Response Limitations

Right now, no one has figured out how to exploit and inject results into public AI models, but "bad" generative responses are being shared on social media as a warning of the perils of poor decisions made in dataset sourcing and training. Unseen in the final AI product is the work reputable companies put into making an "ethical" generative AI service that generates responses matching our perceptions of ethical behavior. Without a training methodology that includes guardrails, generative AI might achieve results that are wholly unethical. Humans try to address this problem by ensuring that incentives are aligned with ethical behavior, but as the Wells Fargo cross-selling scandal[80] demonstrated (and as generative AI will mimic), setting a target outcome might not be achieved in the manner intended.[81]

There are bad actors building generative AI models that explicitly fail to set protections against unethical uses of generative AI such as disinformation propaganda[82] and nonconsensual pornographic images.[83] The rise of prompt engineering or a "grandma hack"[84] that jailbreaks generative AI outside the confines of its configuration has a corollary in the software engineering world via SQL injection attacks. When building and deploying generative AI services, understanding these risks and mitigating them is critical to the successful operation of these tools.

Let's investigate an example within my domain of expertise: software engineering. Suppose a prompt for a piece of software to solve a particular problem returns a working solution. This solution might be devoid of critical considerations that are needed for a final solution; researchers have found that ChatGPT has generated code with viable exploits in it.[85] From my own experience, the availability of software online does not directly correlate to being high-quality and exploit-free. So many reference materials and sample applications are written with the assumption that the engineer will incorporate that functionality within the larger context of security and access controls.

There is a famous open source saying that "with enough eyeballs, all bugs are shallow,"[86] implying that the more people who look at software, the less defects there are in it. We currently don't know the extent to which GitHub or other software repositories are included in training datasets, but what of the software written fifteen years ago with no updates? Exploits are often chain attacks as well, where two sets of code might be fine independently but introduce a vulnerability when combined together in one system. I review this deeper in the section my personal use of ChatGPT, but the key point is that starting with critical analysis of training data will go a long way in your own implementation and adoption of generative AI solutions.

Zero to One Idea Iteration

Generative AI services seem to most benefit the $0 \rightarrow 1$, or first iteration cycle. For every prompt, ChatGPT will provide as many iterations as requested. You can ask the same question repeatedly, and it will happily oblige with a new answer. In my own personal experience, ChatGPT only has so many iterations of ideas before it is no longer able to provide unique insights. I identify this to be around 3-5 cycles.

Revisiting the limitations of training data, it also cannot envision or create brand new concepts because its output is directly based on its inputs. One example I can speak to is the evolution of webpages from the 1990s to now. Each decade has seen an iteration of design patterns that can date a website to a particular era. ChatGPT is happy to provide a semi-modern template for a landing page, but it will not be able to predict future patterns that might be more effective as new devices are invented or browsing habits change, to say nothing of picking a framework or building a new one.

When prompting for new iterations, ChatGPT can get stuck on previous prompts. For example, I asked it to come up with catchy company names with my name in them, and it gave me ten options incorporating my last name. As you can see below, not very creative in my book.

James: "How about 10 business name ideas for 3D printing last name Rowe."

ChatGPT 4o: "Sure thing, James! Here are 10 business name ideas for a 3D printing business incorporating your last name, Rowe:"

1. RowePrint Creations
2. Rowe 3D Solutions
3. RowePrint Innovations
4. RoweFab 3D
5. RowePrint Technologies
6. 3D Rowe Designs
7. RoweCraft 3D
8. RowePrint Works
9. Rowe3D Studio
10. RowePrint Prototypes

The Jobs of Tomorrow

Many economists have looked at how existing jobs will experience displacement, augmentation, and lower barriers to entry. But there is still open speculation as to what the jobs of tomorrow will be. I think we will see some trial and error with jobs, as we saw with the transition of medical record systems from paper to electronic records. Ultimately, generative AI is not a broad transformation like the internet or electricity as some pundits imagine; it depends on large sources of previously published data and can only make predictions based on that dataset.

Impacted knowledge workers will need to learn yet another software system to perform their jobs. Back-office professionals on average work with 5-10+ proprietary software systems, including custom business software, SaaS vendor solutions, and other business productivity tools. These workers will need to augment their workflows with the capabilities of generative AI and especially understand that it differs from a system of records that reflects facts vs. a best-guess product based on training sets.

Just as with the transition to electronic records, new jobs would be invented to help adopt the new systems, support transitioning to them, and curating the training datasets. Validating these models, providing accountability, and conforming to government regulations are other areas that will be invented. There will need to be new roles and responsibilities in both government and business to navigate this information. Knowing which models are trained in certain topics or the best prompts to use to find information are new skills that didn't exist prior to generative AI services. One of the looming challenges is that this rapid rate of change and disruption is going to happen at a pace not seen before and will undermine specific areas of expertise that individuals have spent decades mastering. I visit this later in the myth of retraining appendix item.

Here's a positive example of net job creation and generative AI. Consider a fruit famer who has hundreds of acres of fruit-bearing trees and wants to maximize the yield per acre. Historically, local universities will partner with farmers and crop-growers to help boost yields, and one program uses unmanned aerial vehicles and sensors that go beyond the human spectrum to collect data down to the leaves of individual trees and provide insights to fruit farms.[87]

What previously would be done by walking or driving through an orchard a few times a season can now be done almost continuously. What was done by a handful of experts is now supported by companies that employ their own experts, to say nothing of the work that goes into building and maintaining drones. Before the addition of technology, lower yields were accepted as part of nature. Now, land can be used more effectively and there are more people employed in the pursuit of this yield.

Augmenting Professional Services

Here I refer mainly to my attempts to get answers that I would previously only get from consulting with a lawyer, accountant, or IT professional. In short, I was not able to replace these services, but I could see how in the future, these experts could rely on AI agents to provide context to any given conversation. I would not rely on anything ChatGPT or generative AI has to say on any of these matters. It was able to identify broad themes from my prompts, but I had to do research or pay for a professional answer. Here are some examples summarized.

Estate law and building a will. ChatGPT was happy to outline the various sections of an estate plan, but failed to discern that a living will, health proxy, estate documents, and trusts were all separate parts of an estate plan. I took the 20 or so pages that I drafted as part of my experiment to an estate attorney, who I speculate just tried to restrain from laughing. I suppose it's better than trying to do it totally alone, but ChatGPT felt a poor substitute for completing static templates readily available online. At least a template provided by a professional directly correlates to a completed legal document. A future AI agent might be better at collecting information for said templates, but current AI is unable to draft a comprehensive and legally enforceable estate plan.

IT help with my personal domain mail server. I started to receive error messages that my emails were being flagged as spam. I copied the error message as a prompt to ChatGPT and it responded with a very generic response to check IP Blacklist Status or just use a different email provider. Again, I suppose these are viable options, but dramatically large in scope compared to the final solution. I filed a ticket with my email provider and within minutes, a real human provided me with an answer: I needed to set up DMARC records on my domain. An irony is that the entire ticket support process was littered with calls to use Microsoft's Copilot AI, which was not able to identify the correct solution to my problem. The lesson here is that with enough filed tickets, a generative AI might be able to handle these, but initially it was the human operator who noticed the trend and was very fast at triaging and fixing my issue.

LLC formation and legal documentation. Solidly, hire a lawyer. ChatGPT was able to direct me to the New York state LLC formation details, but again did nothing to bind my work to an LLC or give any other copyright/trademark/patent guidance. When prompted to write articles of incorporation, it got most of the sections, but it was incomplete. The state of New York offers a handy PDF that has all the correct sections described. Again, I would not rely on generative AI for critical business legal documents, nor would I trust it to recreate what is already posted online. I surmise that since generative AI is providing a statistical average response to the prompt, it could never capture the totality of what is already provided as a template flat-fee service by many attorneys.

Accounting and expenses. So many of my accounting questions are currently handled by a fantastic firm I've worked with for many years.

They keep me aware of new laws and regulations, such as the corporate transparency act, and help me stay compliant as a business. Again, you can ask ChatGPT various accounting questions, but nothing substitutes for conversations with these professionals. When prompted for a list of expenses on Schedule C or Schedule F, ChatGPT gets the quantity and majority of the categories correct, but lumps together separate line items as one category; for example, "Interest" has two line items but ChatGPT initially responds with one line. If you prompt it to clarify, it will suddenly "remember" that there are two lines, not one.

James: "Isn't 'interest' two lines, not one?"

ChatGPT: "Yes, you are correct. On Schedule C, 'Interest' is indeed divided into two separate lines."

Now, in the future, all of these professionals might have their own AI models to handle my queries or provide insights based on their geographic area of expertise. But for right now, the humans are winning.

Conclusion

We've explored impacts that generative AI will have on individual workers and businesses. We've looked at early usages and how signs indicate that this new technology will have net benefits for those who are able to understand and employ it. But AI currently lacks oversight or even the semblance of action from American governmental bodies to tackle the thorny issues of privacy, copyright, and ethics surrounding the capture of data, data use in training models, and the deployment of AI to regulated industries such as healthcare, finance, and law. It's my desire that in contributing my own thoughts and observations on the matter, we can focus on the boundaries of advancement that best benefit our society as a whole.

There are some things to start doing today, no matter where you are in your personal journey with generative AI. Review the current state of the AI landscape with reports from Gartner, Havard Business Review, or the Stanford AI Index Report.[88] Evaluate what products and tools are on the market with an eye toward solving an existing problem. Generative AI is a new tool in the proverbial toolbelt that can be applied most effectively to domain areas that have high-quality datasets and with the guidance of an established data governance team.

Never have we seen such a learning- and output-capable system. In addition to the compliance assessments needed to guide building and deploying generative AI products, we also need an ethical framework. What is OK for AI to do, and what needs to be done by a human? Will an AI-infused refrigerator be acceptable but not an AI preschool teacher? Let's revisit some of the metaphors that will hopefully transcend any specific technical approach and be relevant in the future even as this particular set of citations grows stale.

The evolution of generative AI products is following a similar track as the evolution and adoption of GPS or the adoption of new business practices such as electronic medical records or enterprise resource systems in large corporations. Presently we are in the early stages of this innovation, with the first few iterations going from curious toy (ChatGPT-2.5) to serious business tool (JPMorgan Chase AI Agent). While generative AI looks like it will disrupt and augment many digital-based knowledge workers, there are entire industries that it will have much less impact on. Just as GPS applications evolved from military, to geology, then to consumers via smartphone, I predict that generative AI will need to be built for specific purposes and domain areas to be most useful. These new tools are yet to be invented that will fully leverage generative AI in the workplace.

The race between workers and generative AI is also like the fable of John Henry. There is no utility in trying to outcompete the raw output of generative AI products. Whereas before initial brainstorming and problem solving started with a blank page, the outputs from generative AI can achieve an acceptable minimal starting point for some tasks. It is best to understand what generative AI is capable of to find a viable niche for human contribution. The bitter truth is that just as the steam engine devalued physical labor, generative AI will devalue certain cognitive tasks, and the solution to that will require both individual efforts and government intervention.

I predict that data curation and subject matter experts will become more valuable in this economy. Think back to the librarian metaphor: having experts guiding the data curation will provide a check on the hallucination aspects of generative AI. Another value of these experts is in validating predictions; early examples of using generative AI to rapidly generate possible new discoveries yields far too many results for anyone to test and verify.[89] Generative AI will create a new frontier of experts needed to interpret and validate results. For now, AI is still very much limited to the digital realm.

"How will this affect me?" That's a great question—one that I don't have the answer to, and one I think about for myself as well. My greatest desire is that in researching and looking ahead, you'll be able to ride this change in business and society. For those who aren't able to, I look to the government,[90] whose mandate is to protect its citizens by providing regulations and guidance to corporations leveraging this technology. The reality is that no one automatable task is the sum of all tasks needed to complete a workday. For every task that is automated, there will be another that is currently neglected or a new one invented. The question isn't what will happen when work is automated, but how we as a species can add the most utility and value to society.[91]

If all of this seems like it is anti-advancement, please think of it more as pro-thoughtfulness. I can see why so many are excited about the possibilities of this technology to alleviate and reduce the work needed to produce the same goods and services. It will bring new insights and capabilities to governments and organizations that have finite resources. But with great power comes great responsibility, and I hope that through this transition, we can keep our humanity.

More Resources

Because this primer was an overview mainly focused on the impact to American workers and their businesses, there were areas I did not dive deep on. Below I've listed the most comprehensive and informative articles and resources that address these domain areas. If you were to ask "Where can I learn more about X," here is where I would direct you.

Genesis Moment of Generative AI Products

First is a link to the genesis moment for modern generative AI products. This *Wired* article summarizes a whitepaper published by Google engineers titled "Attention Is All You Need." It is the technologies in this whitepaper that form a foundational pillar for all that has come since.

https://www.wired.com/story/eight-google-employees-invented-modern-ai-transformers-paper/

How ChatGPT Works Mathematically

After reading about the genesis moment of generative AI learning, find here a deep dive on how statistics drive generative output. Stephen Wolfram in "What Is ChatGPT Doing and Why Does It Work" does an amazing breakdown of how math is used in generative AI products. He specifically focuses on the language outputs via statistical modeling.

https://writings.stephenwolfram.com/2023/02/what-is-chatgpt-doing-and-why-does-it-work/

Business Consultant and Research Firms

Harvard Business School,[92] Gartner, and McKinsey have comprehensive analyses on AI, and the consensus is that it is a transformative technology with lots of potential but also lots of pending legal challenges. Early studies and anecdotal evidence indicate there is positive ROI on even rudimentary AI implementations.

If the history of big tech provides any guidance, the dust will settle, and the AI companies with the highest-quality data moats and most integrated AI agents will carry the next billion-dollar businesses to market. I've included below two links to industry assessments from Gartner and McKinsey, respectively. Finally, I've linked to an excellent review from a real attorney published in the *Texas Law Review* journal of "fair-use" as it pertains to the gathering of training data.

https://www.gartner.com/en/articles/understand-and-exploit-gen-ai-with-gartner-s-new-impact-radar

https://www.mckinsey.com/capabilities/quantumblack/our-insights/the-state-of-ai

https://texaslawreview.org/fair-learning/

Acknowledgements

I want to acknowledge and thank every single author that I cited in this work and the many more I learned from who took the time to publish their thoughts online. It is thanks to the tireless efforts of real human beings who research, write, and publish their thoughts that this book is possible. Generative AI may be the topic of this book, but generative outputs exist only thanks to original works. Especially, I would like to highlight the fantastic editors and writers at *Wired* magazine— my single largest source of cited materials. In truth, *Wired* has been my go-to trusted source of technical news for decades.

A special thank you to my early readers, friends, and draft feedback providers including Mike, Fred, Erin, Tony, Adam, and Jay. And another person: although I haven't worked with them in decades, I want to thank Bella, who showed me the value of the written word.

Writing is 90 percent rewriting, and it would be foolish of me not to thank the team at The Red to Black Editing Company who were extremely patient with my frequent revisions and provided me tremendously valuable feedback; any errors that remain are my own.

Finally, to mirror my dedication, thank you to my children who patiently afforded me the time to take a passion of researching AI and turn it into a small original work that I hope others will find useful.

About the Author

James Rowe is a software engineering manager with over 20 years of experience in a variety of industries. He has experience as a software engineer, software architect, and people leader with a wide range of technologies. Based in upstate New York, James leads software engineering teams in creating cutting-edge software solutions that drive business growth and innovation.

In this book, James combines his extensive technical knowledge with practical insights, offering readers a firsthand guide to understanding and leveraging AI in business contexts. His clear, approachable writing style and hands-on approach make complex AI concepts accessible to professionals at all levels.

Appendix: Generative AI and Humanity

What does it mean to be human?[93] And why is there so much fretting about a tool that seems to undermine what was long thought to be the domain of humanity: creation? Right now, there needs to be more education on the limitations of generative AI, and regulations are needed to ensure ethical deployment of these solutions.

Given that the outputs from generative AI are smooth, aggregated, and statistically similar, it's worth noting that humans should embrace the aspects of their personalities that make them unique and independent of the summarizing effects of generative AI. It's not so much that generative AI will be the next Robert Frost; at best, it is able to copy the style of Robert Frost. Even with every model advance, generative AI is still bound by its training data and cannot explore ideas that don't already exist.

This brings a very real need for input from the legislative branch of government, which can choose to regulate these tools, relegating them to the realm of just that: tools. With a regulatory ethical framework, we can leverage the productivity gains from generative AI without letting loose a Pandora's box of automation rendering large pools of workers unable to exchange their labor for wages.

Historically, technological innovations have produced winners and losers. One caveat to this sentiment is the speed with which generative AI will move into the market; there is no indication that everyone displaced by these innovations will be able to find like-skilled or like-compensated careers in the time it will take for businesses and governments to adopt them. There have been a variety of proposals, from universal income to 32-hour workweeks, to compensate for the advancements in productivity.

Here I focus on just a few of the questions facing the broad adoption of generative AI. Reid Hoffman has published a great book called *Impromptu: Amplifying Our Humanity Through AI*,[94] which goes over a ton of material on this topic, including a look at major industry domain areas. I think the better question is how the culmination of innovations and research will impact humanity as we strive toward some type of artificial general intelligence.

Many knowledge workers define their existence and utility by the professions they have adopted. "What do you do?" is a common first question when meeting someone. "I am an X" gives a rough outline of a person. They are interested in that domain. They took time to study and excel at it. When a new innovation like generative AI comes along and threatens this pursuit of excellence—undermines livelihoods—it can be unnerving.

It seems that the race between knowledge workers and generative AI mirrors the fable of John Henry and the steam engine. For every one mythical knowledge worker who can beat generative AI, there are many more places of business that just need the proverbial steam engine to extract value from the business process. I think that in the future, humanity will find new ways to add value by either focusing on the things that cannot be completed with generative AI and/or the pursuit of new knowledge that cannot be seen with existing datasets.

Across the studies reviewing generative AI and tasks susceptible to automation and augmentation, there have been areas and domains that require human intervention. Complex problems might appear solvable by generative AI but quickly run into complex social dynamics and the irrational behaviors of human beings. It's one thing to be in a tech-centric bubble and think that a digital solution will upend society, presuming that government or non-digital intervention interrupts the rollout of the technology. Just as the luddites[xvi] found, though, there will be some models destroyed along the way but progress will march on.

The Value of Human Interaction

If the years of COVID isolation taught us anything, it's that there is a human drive to socialize and be around other people. Remote learning and AI agents sound great in practice, but after three years of some form of remote education, we are back in the classrooms, interacting with our peers in pursuit of knowledge.

One aspect unique to humanity is living with the emotional outcomes of a decision. Nothing on the market today has any form of long-term memory. No regrets or second-guessing, no permanent recall. Do we really want AI agents that remember everything?[95] Part of our ability to forget and rewrite our own history of events allows us to move on, to let time heal all wounds.

Another example of automation run amok is with the hiring process experienced by workers, which might include prerecorded sessions or even interviews with chatbots.[96] As a society, are we OK with this

---

xvi. Or as my daughter told me as I was working on this project, "Dad, I'll destroy AI." Thanks sweetie, I believe in you. https://en.wikipedia.org/wiki/Luddite/.

detached process being an acceptable hiring practice? How about the opposite? Are workers who use AI to apply to hundreds of jobs a day acting in an ethical fashion?

In my personal use of AI, I've explored a specific example of asking AI about the placement of the banner at the finish line and its impact on the motivation of runners. In truth, I tried to talk about this question with several of my friends before I turned to ChatGPT. None of them had given it any thought or found it interesting, and I'm sure there are things in their lives that are the same for me. One of the great flattening effects of the internet has been its ability to let us find other people who share similar curiosities, and I think that generative AI-based agents will fill part of this niche.

Testing as a Measure of Human Attainment

The journal *Nature* reports that generative AI is beating most human metrics of attainment and performing at a postgraduate level via test assessments.[97] There is a fascination with generative AI's ability to solve and complete these standardized tests. As you build your understanding that generative AI is based on pattern-matching, it seems much less impressive that it is able to navigate tests for which there are hundreds of thousands of examples and solutions to train on.

The real critical thought here is what does it mean to measure human aptitude? The ability to grasp concepts and apply them to the problem at hand are the critical skills for humanity. Who's to say that the bar exam of the future will focus more on ethics than all the practice areas of law when a generative AI can provide some form of cross-referenced materials? Even without generative AI, some states are looking at the effectiveness of a bar exam and its measure of success for practicing attorneys. Oregon and Washington[98] are evaluating alternative credentialing measures to become a practicing attorney.

In the future, I do hope testing as a measure of human attainment requires the application of critical thought and not a regurgitation of facts or memoranda. What does it mean when AI is able to recite something that might take a student many repetitions to learn? To say nothing of what it takes to be an expert in the field? One study found that completely AI-generated submissions achieved a higher score than humans in 84 percent of assignments.[99] Does this mean AI is "smart" or merely regurgitative?

How can we trust the outputs of a pattern-matching machine? Will future developments in generative AI include the ability to measure how right or wrong it is based on its training material? When will we make the leap from guessing to knowing? I refer mostly to artificial general intelligence (AGI),[100] which is the predicted next iteration of these technologies. Currently though there is no direct proof that advances in LLM based generative AI will result in AGI. There is a mixed consensus on when AGI might emerge from the nascent stage, if this is the precursor to that next leap, with one poll predicting this breakout has a 50 percent chance of occurring in the early 2030s.[101] Even if this occurs, there are mixed thoughts on what AGI would actually look like and what its implications for cognitive-based workers would be.

Because AI is generating statistically correct outputs, recent tools trying to detect AI-generated text are not able to do so reliably. So-claimed "cheating" catching systems like Turnitin pass judgment and declare things AI-written[102] or plagiarized without any systematic way to inspect the process. What's extremely disappointing is that many of these technology companies say, "Oopsie, won't happen again," and blame it on content moderation systems and processes that let through bad actors, with a promise to ban those users—as if that somehow solves the problem.

European Union and the General Data Protection Regulation (GDPR)

This primer takes a very USA-centric perspective on the challenges of leveraging generative AI without clearly identifying all sources of their training data. International companies, especially those that operate within the EU, have to comply with more requirements concerning comprehensive data privacy laws. The EU has released a regulatory framework for AI[103] products that presents a "minimizing harm pyramid" for its citizens.[104] So far, American big tech companies have responded by threatening[105] not to operate in the region,[106] creating a different experience just for EU citizens,[107] or actively lobbying against said regulations.

There is an open question as to the expectations of data privacy and collection by corporations building generative AI services. What is and isn't expected from online platforms and data collection, both as it relates to physical activities in the public square and to online postings for major social networks and smaller self-hosted ones? It is uncanny that corporations can just "update" their terms of service to seemingly and retroactively opt everyone and all content into whatever business purposes they choose. The EU and its regulations are currently at odds with generative AI products, and time will reveal if the end result is better for consumers or other nations.

The United States government seems to have mostly focused on the fact that technology doesn't always do a great job of addressing biases, inequality, and privacy;[108] however, this technology is here and can be used. For every new app with trivial generative AI integrations, the hope is others will be developed to leverage it for new scientific breakthroughs.

Another risk governments will have to evaluate is that if too many workers are displaced by AI, it will reduce overall GDP and impact the labor market in negative ways. If the expectation is that a traditional degree or advanced certificate takes 2-6 years to attain, what does that mean in the interim when these generative AI services are expected to augment large swaths of knowledge workers' capabilities in that same time period?

Critical Thought: Dataset Ethics Regarding Privacy and Uncompensated Creators

When looking at the datasets used for generative AI services, what are the privacy implications of a service that has not proven or provided a way to inspect its training dataset? Are your prompts with generative AI models considered private? What terms of services cover interactions with these services? What about data privacy? We've already seen court cases detail Google search history—what happens when your ChatGPT search history is subpoenaed—or worse, leaked?[109]

Is it possible to opt out of these systems?[110] No, probably not. As Palantir[111] has shown through its direct relationships with police departments, your personal data and likeness are very likely already in training data being used for any number of "solutions." Where is the legislation that protects citizens from being used for commercial products against their ethics? Even the most basic of protections for digital content hosted online, a "robots.txt" file, has no meaningful enforcement mechanism but is based on the honor system.[112]

We have explored the topic of copyright, but another aspect of large training datasets is they are built on the unpaid labor of content moderators and online contributors. GitHub, Stack Overflow, Wikipedia, and Reddit are all cited as primary sources for training models, and all rely on unpaid contributors—to say nothing of hijacking the mission of Wikipedia and the labor and expertise of everyone contributing to those platforms, turning it into a paid product. I don't think any user who voluntarily contributed their knowledge thought to themselves "Yes, one day a robot will copy all my content without attribution, compensation, or recognition."

Let's look at the example of Audible recently releasing of over 40,000 AI-generated textbook readings.[113] Does this improve accessibility? Yes, but it takes potential work away from human narrators. Would these books ever have been narrated without the use of AI? Text-to-audio technologies have been available for decades; was it the scale that was too much? Who owns the rights to these audio versions? And most importantly, what training data was used to produce the spoken versions of the books?

There are some companies[114] trying to determine the usefulness of a generative AI service trained on known public domain works, but the key takeaway is that in addition to the copyright concerns of digital data, there are the ethical ones. Working to establish data governance and uncovering these latent liability issues during vendor analysis are import aspects to consider going forward.

Appendix: Personal Use of AI via ChatGPT Thus Far

Looking at my personal history of use with ChatGPT over the past roughly 18 months, I find a number of interesting responses that didn't fit any of the core sections of this book, which I am including here for reference. I can say that I found model 2.x fun to experiment with, but I quickly returned to traditional web searches to find what I was looking for. With the launch of the 3.5 model, I made a conscious effort to leverage it in lieu of traditional search, but the model's response rate was too slow, and it wasn't able to produce the "right" answers to specific prompts. At the time, ChatGPT was unable to scan the internet for new information or link out to other resources. This will rapidly evolve as generative AI services figure out how to serve the needs of their customers and answer prompts accurately.

The release of the ChatGPT-4o model really upped the game on several fronts. Prompts could now be sent via picture, and attempts were made to address some of the citation issues, but it hasn't been perfect. After about a month, I am still returning to Google (or rather, DuckDuckGo) to find things, and primary sources can still provide better guidance than generative AI.

However, ChatGPT-4o has excelled at a number of things, which I've detailed below. In the writing and research of this book, I've used it for about a hundred "threads," made use of the downloaded iPhone and Mac apps, and I find myself using ChatGPT first instead of traditional search about 20-30 percent of the time. A cursory look at my search history verifies this with a roughly 20 percent drop in native DuckDuckGo searches. I have not analyzed how often I started with ChatGPT but then switched to traditional search, which still occurs enough to be worth noting.

ChatGPT-4o as a Buying Agent

One of the longest running "conversations" I've had with ChatGPT-4o is asking it to analyze listings of digital cameras. What I really like about the process is that I can just send it a screenshot of a listing and ChatGPT is able to figure out what it is looking at, cross-reference it with product details, and tell me if it matches my desired criteria.

It has made insightful observations based on previous conversations —for example, when an analyzed model doesn't have 4k video or uses a fixed-lens style that wouldn't be compatible with my other equipment I've shared in the process, it highlights it might not meet my needs. I've used this same process to evaluate 3D printers and other items I don't have a lot of firsthand knowledge about. It shortcuts all of the product research of looking through product manuals, review sites, and trying to match this new product against my desired functionality. ChatGPT-4o is even able to give me links out to shopping sites such as eBay and Amazon— something it couldn't do previously.

See the below image, an example of where I've shown ChatGPT a screenshot of a used camera package off Marketplace. You can see the market comparison, and it was able to correctly identify the model. I've tried this with posts that don't list the model, and ChatGPT-4o has done a reliable job of identifying the correct model.

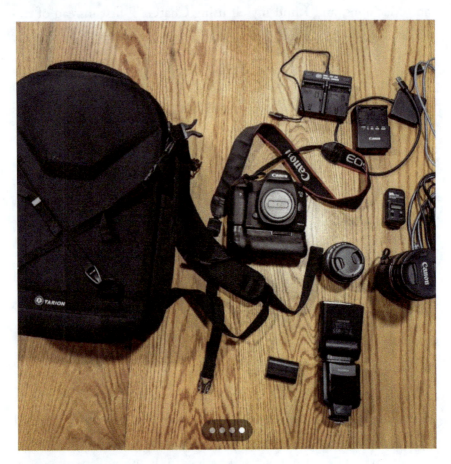

Canon 5D MK3 Package
$800 ~~$1,500~~

James: "What about this bundle?"

ChatGPT-4o: "The Canon 5D Mark III is an excellent camera, though it doesn't offer 4K video recording, which might be a consideration if 4K is a priority for you … For $800, this bundle is a good deal if you don't need 4K video. However, if 4K recording is important, you might want to stick with a more recent model like the Canon EOS R6."

Where it fails as a valuable AI agent, though, is its inability to provide me with a summary of everything I've asked it, or tell me what it would recommend to me from session to session. While I hypothesize AI agents will get better in the future, right now, when I prompt ChatGPT for a summary of all the camera models I've shown it (more than a dozen), it is only able to return a list of four items and a poor summary of their qualities (which I've omitted).

James: "Can you give me a list of every camera model I've sent you?"

ChatGPT-4o: "Here's a list of the camera models you've sent, along with the date, price, and pros and cons discussed:"

1. **Canon 5D Mark III Package**
2. **Canon SL2 Rebel**
3. **Sony HDR-CX405**
4. **Canon T3i Kit**

Image Prompting and Exploring Novel Ideas

Decades ago, my grandfather wrote the physics department at our local university to ask, "What is faster, feet first or hands first baseball base slide?" They answered, with a complete paper. Similarly, librarians help navigate their vast knowledge collections. There will be questions and thoughts that you might want to explore that no one in your circle might want to discuss. Here's mine: Does the placement of the banner for the finish of a race impact the outcomes for the runners?

I jotted a quick diagram in my notebook and asked ChatGPT what it thought. This was my personal "wow" moment. ChatGPT was able to parse my diagram and offer its own "thoughts" on the matter.

James: "I have a random thought. What do you think?"

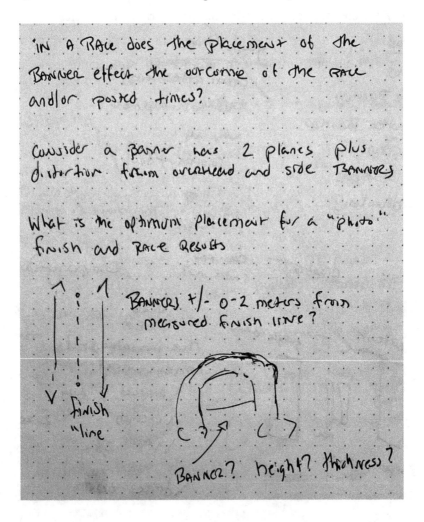

ChatGPT-4o: "Your random thought about the placement of the banner in a race and its impact on the outcome and posted times is intriguing! ... By ensuring the banner is placed optimally, you can maintain accuracy in race results and provide a clear finish line for both participants and spectators."

DALL-E and Image Generation

Of the hundred or so prompts with ChatGPT, only a handful pertain to generating images, mostly humorous "preview" social images for my personal GitHub repositories and generating fun sticker ideas and images for LinkedIn posts. I don't feel like I'm taking any work away from professional creatives, as previously, I would've just left them blank, or made some MS Paint-inspired clip art.

In fact, quite the opposite: generally, one of the first steps as a client is to "describe" what you want. What better way to start that conversation than having samples of images that are close? The image creation is almost a teaser. Some of the generated images are almost there, and make me want to find a designer to finish the work started. Again, currently the copyright office is crystal clear: you cannot copyright images generated by AI. So long as that's the case, I foresee humans remaining involved in the creative process.

Previously, one of the biggest limitations with images was text in the image, but that seems to have been fixed with one or two words in ChatGPT-4o. However, right now, ChatGPT has a very hard time creating very small iterations of the same image. It seems to create an entirely new image even with a prompt to keep all things the same. Here's a very straightforward example of generating an image of a book. Each requested change generates a totally "new" book from my perspective.

James: "Create a small image of a book."

James: "Make the book cover red."

James: "What happened to the bookmark?"

ChatGPT-4o: "It looks like the original prompt didn't include a bookmark, but let's add one now. I'll generate an image with a red book cover and a visible bookmark.

"Let me update the prompt and generate the new image."

James: "Now add a title 'AI Book.'"

As a Replacement to Traditional Search

It's been twenty years since Google designed a simple, better search experience for users; the last few years have seen the first page of search results become all ads and/or low-value SEO sites—so much so that appending "Reddit" to the search query is a common tactic to try and find authentic content. One of the joys of using something like

ChatGPT is the dramatically improved ability to find answers to simple queries.

Here's an example: I was in the grocery story wondering if rosemary or bay leaves would improve the flavor of my sauce. Simple; an answer in less than 20 seconds.

James: "Bay leaves or rosemary for meat sauce?"

ChatGPT-4o: "Bay leaves for a more subtle, earthy flavor that enhances the overall taste without overpowering it. Rosemary can be a bit strong and might dominate the sauce."

Contrast that with trying to find the same answer on Google (or DuckDuckGo). Not only do I not find an answer to my question, but I'm overwhelmed with recipes. That's not what I asked for. I wanted to know which spice would improve my sauce. Clicking on either of the first two links leads to a site covered with ads, and neither had an answer to my question.

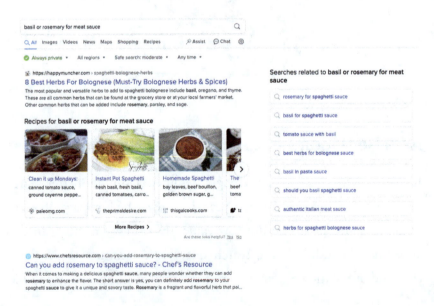

Ultimately, a search starts with a quest to find something, and the tool that delivers the most effective answer wins. Others have written about how search results are suffering from "enshittification"[115] that renders them less and less useful.

This is not a new problem in the use of scraping and scanning digital data. Search engine optimized content has plagued search results now for over a decade.[116] Typically, these sites are ad-laden and offer little substance in exchange for their high rankings in search results. One type of egregious offender I can think of are sites that repost obituaries or lawyer/doctor profiles, which are frequently out of date or provide services that don't directly connect users with their desired search results.

I recognize that not everyone publishes content for free, and hosting said content does cost money. So how do we honor copyrighted works and provide an incentive to produce more? Is the future of writing to join an AI writing pool to generate new content? Dare I say cookbooks will make a return as a way to provide revenue to authors and a great experience to users?

James Rowe

James Rowe

Endnotes

1. Sarah Kessler, "The AI Revolution Will Change Work. Nobody Agrees How," *New York Times*, June 10, 2023, https://www.nytimes.com/2023/06/10/business/ai-jobs-work.html/.

2. I think we are in the innovation trigger cycle. Expectations continue to inflate with each news cycle. https://en.wikipedia.org/wiki/Technology_adoption_life_cycle/; Lori Perri, "What's New in Artificial Intelligence from the 2023 Gartner Hype Cycle," *Gartner*, August 17, 2023, https://www.gartner.com/en/articles/what-s-new-in-artificial-intelligence-from-the-2023-gartner-hype-cycle/.

3. Air Canada forced to honor chatbot response to its policies online. Moffatt v. Air Canada, 2024 BCCRT 149 (2024), https://www.canlii.org/en/bc/bccrt/doc/2024/2024bccrt149/2024bccrt149.html/.

4. Cade Metz, "In Two Moves, AlphaGo and Lee Sedol Redefined the Future," *Wired*, March 16, 2016, https://www.wired.com/2016/03/two-moves-alphago-lee-sedol-redefined-future/.

5. The University of Toronto's AI Index Report 2024 suggests that 63 percent of respondents were aware of ChatGPT. Of those aware, around half reported using ChatGPT at least once weekly.

6. https://x.com/OpenAI/, used primarily as a timeline of events.

7. Dmitri Brereton, "Google Search Is Dying," *DKB Blog*, February 15, 2022, https://dkb.blog/p/google-search-is-dying/; or this one: Elizabeth Lopatto, "The Ask Jeeves-ification of Online Search," *The Verge*, May 12, 2023, https://www.theverge.com/2023/5/12/23721323/ask-jeeves-remember-when-google-search-worked-ai/. Both cite SEO content farms, ads taking over screen real estate, and just plain not finding what you're looking for as problems for traditional search.

8. Apple press release, "Introducing Apple Intelligence," *Newsroom*, June 10, 2024, https://www.apple.com/newsroom/2024/06/introducing-apple-intelligence-for-iphone-ipad-and-mac/.

9. Colette Stallbaumer, "Introducing Copilot for Microsoft 365—A Whole New Way to Work," *Microsoft 365* (blog), March 16, 2023, https://www.microsoft.com/en-us/microsoft-365/blog/2023/03/16/introducing-microsoft-365-copilot-a-whole-new-way-to-work/.

10. Sundar Pichai, "An Important Next Step on Our AI Journey," *The Keyword* (blog), *Google*, February 6, 2023, https://blog.google/technology/ai/bard-google-ai-search-updates/.

11. "Meet Your New Assistant: Meta AI, Built with Llama 3," *Meta Newsroom* (blog), April 18, 2024, https://about.fb.com/news/2024/04/meta-ai-assistant-built-with-llama-3/.

12. Lori Perri, "Understand and Exploit GenAI with Gartner's New Impact Radar," *Gartner*, December 21, 2023, https://www.gartner.com/en/articles/understand-and-exploit-gen-ai-with-gartner-s-new-impact-radar/.

13. Alex Singla et al., "The State of AI in Early 2024: Gen AI Adoption Spikes and Starts to Generate Value," *QuantumBlack AI by McKinsey*, May 30, 2024, https://www.mckinsey.com/capabilities/quantumblack/our-insights/the-state-of-ai#/

14. "70% of Workers Using ChatGPT at Work Are Not Telling Their Boss; Overall usage among Professionals Jumps to 43%," *fishbowl*, February 1, 2023, https://www.fishbowlapp.com/insights/70-percent-of-workers-using-chatgpt-at-work-are-not-telling-their-boss/.

15. Sam Sabin, "Companies Are Struggling to Keep Corporate Secrets out of ChatGPT," *Axios*, March 10, 2023, https://www.axios.com/2023/03/10/chatgpt-ai-cybersecurity-secrets/.

16. Zoe Thomas, "Bosses Are Trying to Learn Exactly What AI Can Do," in *Tech News Briefing*, produced by the *Wall Street Journal*, podcast, 11:09, https://www.wsj.com/podcasts/tech-news-briefing/bosses-are-trying-to-learn-exactly-what-ai-can-do/7fe982b4-53ad-439a-bc8f-79703bc6e4a6/.

17. David F. Carr, "Stack Overflow Is ChatGPT Casualty: Traffic Down 14% in March," *similarweb*, April 19, 2023, https://www.similarweb.com/blog/insights/ai-news/stack-overflow-chatgpt/.

18. https://stackoverflow.com/help/gen-ai-policy/. No AI allowed.

19. Prashanth Chandrasekar, "Announcing OverflowAI," (blog), *Stack Overflow*, July 27, 2023, https://stackoverflow.blog/2023/07/27/announcing-overflowai/.

20. Sarah Min, "Chegg Shares Drop More than 40% after Company Says ChatGPT Is Killing Its Business," *CNBC*, May 2, 2023, https://www.cnbc.com/2023/05/02/chegg-drops-more-than-40percent-after-saying-chatgpt-is-killing-its-business.html/.

21. How modern AI services are built and delivered: Steven Levy, "8 Google Employees Invented Modern AI. Here's the Inside Story," *Wired*, March

28, 2024, https://www.wired.com/story/eight-google-employees-invented-modern-ai-transformers-paper/.

22. This is the most authoritative deep dive into the statistical workings of ChatGPT and LLM that I've found: Stephen Wolfram, "What Is ChatGPT Doing … and Why Does It Work?," *Stephen Wolfram Writings*, February 14, 2023, https://writings.stephenwolfram.com/2023/02/what-is-chatgpt-doing-and-why-does-it-work/.

23. This is my biggest feature request for ChatGPT: ability to toggle these values for the same prompt. Novita.ai, "What Are Large Language Model Settings: Temperature, Top P and Max Tokens," *Novita AI*, April 29, 2024, https://blogs.novita.ai/what-are-large-language-model-settings-temperature-top-p-and-max-tokens/.

24. Smart Compose was released circa 2018. Paul Lambert, "Write Emails Faster with Smart Compose in Gmail," *The Keyword*, May 8, 2018, https://blog.google/products/gmail/subject-write-emails-faster-smart-compose-gmail/.

25. Jared Kaplan et al., "Scaling Laws for Neural Language Models," *OpenAI*, January 23, 2020, https://openai.com/index/scaling-laws-for-neural-language-models/.

26. Because Reddit data is also the source of bad search results, I would question some of this logic. Kyle Orland, "Reddit Cashes in on AI Gold Rush with $203M in LLM Training License Fees," *Ars Technica*, February 23, 2024, https://arstechnica.com/ai/2024/02/reddit-has-already-booked-203m-in-revenue-licensing-data-for-ai-training/.

27. Natalie Sherman, "World's Biggest Music Labels Sue over AI Copyright," *BBC*, June 25, 2024, https://www.bbc.com/news/articles/ckrrr8yelzvo/.

28. Rachel Goodman, "Why Amazon's Automated Hiring Tool Discriminated against Women," *ACLU News & Commentary*, October 12, 2018, https://www.aclu.org/news/womens-rights/why-amazons-automated-hiring-tool-discriminated-against/.

29. Khari Johnson, "DALL-E 2 Creates Incredible Images—and Biased Ones You Don't See," *Wired*, May 5, 2022, https://www.wired.com/story/dall-e-2-ai-text-image-bias-social-media/.

30. Liv McMahon, "Glue Pizza and Eat Rocks: Google AI Search Errors Go Viral," *BBC*, May 24, 2024, https://www.bbc.com/news/articles/cd11gzejgz4o/.

31. https://en.wikipedia.org/wiki/False_memory#Mandela_effect/.

32. Barry Schwartz, "George Bush 'Miserable Failure' Google Bomb Back, This Time in Knowledge Graph," *Search Engine Land*, June 12, 2013, https://searchengineland.com/george-bush-knowledge-graph-miserable-failure-163009/.

33. Benjamin Hoffman, "First Came 'Spam.' Now, with AI, We've Got 'Slop,'" *New York Times*, June 11, 2024, https://www.nytimes.com/2024/06/11/style/ai-search-slop.html/.

34. Emanuel Maiberg, "Google Books Is Indexing AI-Generated Garbage," *404*, April 4, 2024, https://www.404media.co/google-books-is-indexing-ai-generated-garbage/.

35. Nidhi Subbaraman, "Flood of Fake Science Forces Multiple Journal Closures," *Wall Street Journal*, May 14, 2024, https://www.wsj.com/science/academic-studies-research-paper-mills-journals-publishing-f5a3d4bc/.

36. Jason Koebler, "Facebook's Algorithm Is Boosting AI Spam that Links to AI-Generated, Ad-Laden Click Farms," *404*, March 19, 2024, https://www.404media.co/facebooks-algorithm-is-boosting-ai-spam-that-links-to-ai-generated-ad-laden-click-farms/.

37. Ilia Shumailov et al., "AI Models Collapse When Trained on Recursively Generated Data," *Nature* 631 (2024): 755-759, https://www.nature.com/articles/s41586-024-07566-y/.

38. Trishla Ostwal, "Judge Rules GenAI Content Does Not Have Copyright Protection," *Adweek*, August 22, 2023, https://www.adweek.com/programmatic/judge-rules-genai-content-does-not-have-copyright-protection/.

39. House of Lords Communications and Digital Select Committee Inquiry: Large Language Models, "OpenAI—Written Evidence," https://committees.parliament.uk/writtenevidence/126981/pdf/

40. Mariella Moon, "OpenAI Admits It's Impossible to Train Generative AI without Copyrighted Materials," *Engadget*, January 9, 2024, https://www.engadget.com/openai-admits-its-impossible-to-train-generative-ai-without-copyrighted-materials-103311496.html/.

41. Hayden Field, "Researchers Tested Leading AI Models for Copyright Infringement Using Popular Books, GPT-4 Performed Worst," *CNBC*, March 6, 2024, https://www.cnbc.com/2024/03/06/gpt-4-researchers-tested-leading-ai-models-for-copyright-infringement.html/.

42. Winston Cho, "Big Tech Launches Campaign to Defend AI Use," *Hollywood Reporter*, June 6, 2024, https://www.hollywoodreporter.com/business/business-news/big-tech-lobby-ai-use-1235916540/.

43. Gil Appel, Juliana Neelbauer, and David A. Schweidel, "Generative AI Has an Intellectual Property Problem," *Harvard Business Review*, April 7, 2023, https://hbr.org/2023/04/generative-ai-has-an-intellectual-property-problem/.

44. Chloe Veltman, "Thousands of Authors Urge AI Companies to Stop Using Work without Permission," *NPR*, July 17, 2023, https://www.npr.org/2023/07/17/1187523435/thousands-of-authors-urge-ai-companies-to-stop-using-work-without-permission/.

45. James Vincent, "Getty Images Is Suing the Creators of AI Art Tool Stable Diffusion for Scraping Its Content," *The Verge*, January 17, 2023, https://

www.theverge.com/2023/1/17/23558516/ai-art-copyright-stable-diffusion-getty-images-lawsuit/.

46. "Most specifically, in their training data. And as both research and the proliferation of litigation have shown, current large language models have borne bitter fruit from their tainted seed." Kate Knibbs, "Here's Proof You Can Train an AI Model Without Slurping Copyrighted Content," *Wired*, March 28, 2024, https://www.wired.com/story/proof-you-can-train-ai-without-slurping-copyrighted-content/.

47. Michael M. Grynbaum and Ryan Mac, "The *Times* Sues OpenAI and Microsoft over AI Use of Copyrighted Work," *New York Times*, December 27, 2023, https://www.nytimes.com/2023/12/27/business/media/new-york-times-open-ai-microsoft-lawsuit.html/.

48. Capgemini, *Harnessing the Value of Generative AI: Top Use Cases across Industries* (2023), https://prod.ucwe.capgemini.com/wp-content/uploads/2023/07/Final-Web-Version-Report-Harnessing-the-Value-of-Gen-AI.1.pdf.

49. John Butters, "Highest Number of S&P 500 Companies Citing 'AI' on Earnings Calls over Past 10 years," *FactSet*, May 24, 2024, https://insight.factset.com/highest-number-of-sp-500-companies-citing-ai-on-earnings-calls-over-past-10-years/.

50. Will Knight, "No One Actually Knows How AI Will Affect Jobs," *Wired*, April 11, 2024, https://www.wired.com/story/ai-impact-on-work-mary-daly-interview/.

51. Paul Colford, "A Leap Forward in Quarterly Earnings Stories," *AP*, June 30, 2014, https://blog.ap.org/announcements/a-leap-forward-in-quarterly-earnings-stories/.

52. World Economic Forum, *Jobs of Tomorrow: Large Language Models and Jobs* (2023), https://www.weforum.org/publications/jobs-of-tomorrow-large-language-models-and-jobs/.

53. Sinazo Sibisi and Gys Kappers, "Onboarding Can Make or Break a new Hire's Experience," *Harvard Business Review*, April 5, 2022, https://hbr.org/2022/04/onboarding-can-make-or-break-a-new-hires-experience/.

54. Janakiram MSV, "JPMorgan Chase Leads AI Revolution in Finance with Launch of LLM Suite," *Forbes*, July 30, 2024, https://www.forbes.com/sites/janakirammsv/2024/07/30/jpmorgan-chase-leads-ai-revolution-in-finance-with-launch-of-llm-suite/.

55. Erik Brynjolfsson, Danielle Li, and Lindsey R. Raymond, "Generative AI at Work," *National Bureau of Economic Research* working paper 31161 (2023), https://www.nber.org/system/files/working_papers/w31161/w31161.pdf/.

56. David De Cremer and Garry Kasparov, "AI Should Augment Human Intelligence, Not Replace It," *Harvard Business Review*, March 18, 2021, https://hbr.org/2021/03/ai-should-augment-human-intelligence-not-replace-it/.

57. Brian Welk, "Will AI Make Hollywood Production Cheaper? Don't Count on It," *IndieWire*, May 20, 2024, https://www.indiewire.com/news/business/will-ai-make-hollywood-production-cheaper-1235006290/.

58. David Streitfeld, "If AI Can Do Your Job, Maybe It Can Also Replace Your CEO," *New York Times*, May 28, 2024, https://www.nytimes.com/2024/05/28/technology/ai-chief-executives.html/.

59. Klarna, "Klarna AI Assistant Handles Two-Thirds of Customer Service Chats in Its First Month," *Klarna*, February 27, 2024, https://www.klarna.com/international/press/klarna-ai-assistant-handles-two-thirds-of-customer-service-chats-in-its-first-month/.

60. Rob Thubron, "CEO Replaces 90% of Support Staff with AI, Praises the System on Twitter," *Techspot*, July 12, 2023, https://www.techspot.com/news/99369-ceo-replaces-90-support-staff-ai-praises-system.html/.

61. Rob Thubron, "Generative AI Could Soon Decimate the Call Center Industry, Says CEO," *Techspot*, April 23, 2024, https://www.techspot.com/news/102749-generative-ai-could-soon-decimate-call-center-industry.html/.

62. Newsroom, "Customer Service and Support Leaders Should Assess Generative AI Technology Options to Enhance Their Organization's Function," *Gartner*, August 3, 2023, https://www.gartner.com/en/newsroom/press-releases/2023-08-03-customer-service-and-support-leaders-should-assess-generative-ai-technology-options-to-enhance-their-organizations-function/.

63. Marisa Garcia, "What Air Canada Lost in 'Remarkable' Lying AI Chatbot Case," *Forbes*, February 19, 2024, https://www.forbes.com/sites/marisagarcia/2024/02/19/what-air-canada-lost-in-remarkable-lying-ai-chatbot-case/.

64. Chris Williams, "Keep Your Firm Far Away from Whatever AI Chevy Was Using," *Above the Law*, January 5, 2024, https://abovethelaw.com/2024/01/keep-your-firm-far-away-from-whatever-ai-chevy-was-using/.

65. Jordyn Holman, "At Target, Store Workers Become AI Conduits," *New York Times*, June 20, 2024, https://www.nytimes.com/2024/06/20/business/target-retail-ai.html/.

66. Wes Davis, "McDonald's Will Stop Testing AI to Take Drive-Thru Orders, for Now," *The Verge*, June 16, 2024, https://www.theverge.com/2024/6/16/24179679/mcdonalds-ending-ai-chatbot-drive-thru-ordering-test-ibm/.

67. Joseph Cox, "Inside the Underground Site Where 'Neural Networks' Churn out Fake IDs," *404*, February 5, 2024, https://www.404media.co/inside-the-underground-site-where-ai-neural-networks-churns-out-fake-ids-onlyfake/.

68. Nishtha Badgamia, "Hong Kong Firm Loses over $25mn after Employee's Video Call with Deepfake 'Chief Financial Officer,' Others," *WION*, February 4, 2024, https://www.wionews.com/technology/hong-kong-office-employee-

loses-more-than-25-million-after-video-call-with-deepfake-chief-financial-officer-686908/.

69. https://en.wikipedia.org/wiki/British_Post_Office_scandal/.

70. Sara Merken, "New York Lawyers Sanctioned for Using Fake ChatGPT Cases in Legal Brief," *Reuters*, June 26, 2023, https://www.reuters.com/legal/new-york-lawyers-sanctioned-using-fake-chatgpt-cases-legal-brief-2023-06-22/.

71. Fabrizio Dell'Acqua et al., "Navigating the Jagged Technological Frontier: Field Experimental Evidence of the Effects of AI on Knowledge Worker Productivity and Quality" (working paper, Harvard Business School Technology & Operations Mgt. Unit, 2023).

72. Brynjolfsson et al., "Generative AI at Work."

73. Will Knight, "Chatbot Teamwork Makes the AI Dream Work," *Wired*, June 6, 2024, https://www.wired.com/story/chatbot-teamwork-makes-the-ai-dream-work/.

74. Nilay Patel, "The CEO of Zoom Wants AI Clones in Meetings," *The Verge*, June 3, 2024, https://www.theverge.com/2024/6/3/24168733/zoom-ceo-ai-clones-digital-twins-videoconferencing-decoder-interview/.

75. Jack Nicas and Zach Wichter, "A Worry for Some Pilots: Their Hands-On Flying Skills are Lacking," *New York Times*, March 14, 2019, https://www.nytimes.com/2019/03/14/business/automated-planes.html/.

76. Dave Gershgorn, "GitHub's Automatic Coding Tool Rests on Untested Legal Ground," *The Verge*, July 7, 2021, https://www.theverge.com/2021/7/7/22561180/github-copilot-legal-copyright-fair-use-public-code/.

77. https://github.com/jsr6720/goodreads-csv-to-md/.

78. https://github.com/jsr6720/wordpress-html-scraper-to-md/.

79. Thomas Claburn, "DARPA Suggests Turning Old C Code Automatically into Rust—Using AI, of Course," *The Register*, August 3, 2024, https://www.theregister.com/2024/08/03/darpa_c_to_rust/.

80. https://en.wikipedia.org/wiki/Wells_Fargo_cross-selling_scandal/.

81. https://docs.google.com/spreadsheets/u/1/d/e/2PACX-1vRPiprOaC3H-sCf5Tuum8bRfzYUiKLRqJmbOoC-32JorNdfyTiRRsR7Ea5eWtvsWzuxo8b-jOxCG84dAg/pubhtml/. This is a list of how AI tools have circumvented video game constraints to achieve high scores in what would loosely be considered "nontraditional" means. When the objective is "achieve the highest score," models are optimized to that outcome, regardless of the path taken.

82. David Gilbert, "Neo-Nazis Are All-In on AI," *Wired*, June 20, 2024, https://www.wired.com/story/neo-nazis-are-all-in-on-ai/.

83. Adi Robertson, "Lawmakers Propose Anti-Nonconsensual AI Porn Bill after Taylor Swift Controversy," *The Verge*, January 30, 2024, https://www.

theverge.com/2024/1/30/24056385/congress-defiance-act-proposed-ban-nonconsensual-ai-porn/.

84. "ChatGPT Grandma Exploit," thread on Hacker News, April 19, 2023, https://news.ycombinator.com/item?id=35630801/.

85. Hammond Pearce et al., "Asleep at the Keyboard? Assessing the Security of GitHub Copilot's Code Contributions," *2022 IEEE Symposium on Security and Privacy*, https://arxiv.org/pdf/2108.09293/.

86. https://en.wikipedia.org/wiki/Linus's_law

87. Long He, Sultan Mahmud, and Tyler Shannon, "Unmanned Aerial Vehicle-Based Crop Scouting in Fruit Trees," *PennState Extension*, June 10, 2024, https://extension.psu.edu/unmanned-aerial-vehicle-based-crop-scouting-in-fruit-trees/.

88. Stanford University, *The AI Index Report* (2024), https://aiindex.stanford.edu/report/.

89. Amil Merchant, Simon Batzner, Samuel S. Schoenholz, Muratahan Aykol, Gowoon Cheon, and Ekin Dogus Cubuk, "Scaling Deep Learning for Materials Discovery," *Nature* no. 624 (2023): 80-85, https://www.nature.com/articles/s41586-023-06735-9/.

90. White House Briefing Room, "Vice President Harris Announces OMB Policy to Advance Governance, Innovation, and Risk Management in Federal Agencies' Use of Artificial Intelligence," *White House*, March 28, 2024, https://www.whitehouse.gov/briefing-room/statements-releases/2024/03/28/fact-sheet-vice-president-harris-announces-omb-policy-to-advance-governance-innovation-and-risk-management-in-federal-agencies-use-of-artificial-intelligence/.

91. Sarah Kessler, "The AI Revolution Will Change Work. Nobody Agrees How," *New York Times*, June 10, 2023, https://www.nytimes.com/2023/06/10/business/ai-jobs-work.html/.

92. Dell'Acqua et al., "Jagged Technological Frontier."

93. Bill Gates, "The Age of AI Has Begun," *GatesNotes*, March 21, 2023, https://www.gatesnotes.com/The-Age-of-AI-Has-Begun/.

94. Reid Hoffman and GPT-4, *Impromptu: Amplifying Our Humanity through AI* (Dallepedia, 2023), https://www.impromptubook.com/wp-content/uploads/2023/03/impromptu-rh.pdf

95. Molly Glick, "Facebook Is Filled with AI-Generated Garbage—and Older Adults Are Being Tricked," *Daily Beast*, March 24, 2024, https://www.thedailybeast.com/how-seniors-are-falling-for-ai-generated-pics-on-facebook/.

96. Amanda Hoover, "An AI Cartoon May Interview You for Your Next Job," *Wired*, June 7, 2024, https://www.wired.com/story/ai-cartoon-next-job/.

97. Nicola Jones, "AI Now Beats Humans at Basic Tasks—New Benchmarks Are Needed, Says Major Report," *Nature*, April 15, 2024, https://www.nature.com/articles/d41586-024-01087-4/.

98. Emma Epperly, "Supreme Court: Bar Exam Will No Longer Be Required to Become Attorney in Washington State," *Spokesman-Review*, March 15, 2024, https://www.spokesman.com/stories/2024/mar/15/supreme-court-bar-exam-will-no-longer-be-required-/.

99. Peter Scarfe, Kelly Watcham, Alasdair Clarke, and Etienne Roesch, "A Real-World Test of Artificial Intelligence Infiltration of a University Examinations System: A 'Turing Test' Case Study," *PLoS ONE* 19, no. 6 (2024): e0305354, https://doi.org/10.1371/journal.pone.0305354/.

100. Leopold Aschenbrenner, *Situational Awareness: The Decade Ahead* (2024), https://situational-awareness.ai/wp-content/uploads/2024/06/situationalawareness.pdf/.

101. Will Henshall, "When Might AI Outsmart Us? It Depends Who You Ask," *Time*, January 19, 2024, https://time.com/6556168/when-ai-outsmart-humans/.

102. Miles Klee, "She Was Falsely Accused of Cheating with AI—and She Won't Be the Last," *Rolling Stone*, June 6, 2023, https://www.rollingstone.com/culture/culture-features/student-accused-ai-cheating-turnitin-1234747351/.

103. Directorate-General for Communications Networks, Content and Technology, "AI Act," *Shaping Europe's Digital Future*, June 19, 2024, https://digital-strategy.ec.europa.eu/en/policies/regulatory-framework-ai/.

104. European Parliament, "EU AI Act: First Regulation on Artificial Intelligence," June 8, 2023, https://www.europarl.europa.eu/topics/en/article/20230601STO93804/eu-ai-act-first-regulation-on-artificial-intelligence/.

105. James Vincent, "OpenAI Says It Could 'Cease Operating' in the EU if It Can't Comply with Future Regulation," *The Verge*, May 25, 2023, https://www.theverge.com/2023/5/25/23737116/openai-ai-regulation-eu-ai-act-cease-operating/.

106. Ben Lovejoy, "Withholding Apple Intelligence from EU a 'Stunning Declaration' of Anticompetitive Behavior," *9to5Mac*, June 28, 2024, https://9to5mac.com/2024/06/28/withholding-apple-intelligence-from-eu/.

107. Kacey Lemieux, "EU Data Boundary for the Microsoft Cloud," *Security, Compliance, and Identity* (blog), *Microsoft*, May 6, 2021, https://techcommunity.microsoft.com/t5/security-compliance-and-identity/eu-data-boundary-for-the-microsoft-cloud-frequently-asked/ba-p/2329098/.

108. White House, "Fact Sheet: Vice President Harris Announces OMB Policy to Advance Governance, Innovation, and Risk Management in Federal Agencies' Use of Artificial Intelligence," March 28, 2024, https://www.whitehouse.gov/briefing-room/statements-releases/2024/03/28/fact-sheet-vice-president-

harris-announces-omb-policy-to-advance-governance-innovation-and-risk-management-in-federal-agencies-use-of-artificial-intelligence/

109. Ben Derico, "ChatGPT Bug Leaked Users' Conversation Histories," *BBC*, March 22, 2023, https://www.bbc.com/news/technology-65047304/.

110. Matt Burgess and Reece Rogers, "How to Stop Your Data from Being Used to Train AI," *Wired*, April 10, 2024, https://www.wired.com/story/how-to-stop-your-data-from-being-used-to-train-ai/.

111. Ali Winston, "Palantir Has Secretly Been Using New Orleans to Test Its Predictive Policing Technology" *The Verge*, February 27, 2018, https://www.theverge.com/2018/2/27/17054740/palantir-predictive-policing-tool-new-orleans-nopd/.

112. David Pierce, "The Text File that Runs the Internet," *The Verge*, February 14, 2024, https://www.theverge.com/24067997/robots-txt-ai-text-file-web-crawlers-spiders/.

113. Zo Ahmed, "40,000 AI-Narrated Audiobooks Flood Audible, Dividing Authors and Listeners," *TechSpot*, May 6, 2024, https://www.techspot.com/news/102875-40000-ai-narrated-audiobooks-flood-audible-dividing-authors.html/.

114. kl3m.ai, "KL3M Is the First Fairly Trained LLM," *273Ventures*, March 20, 2024, https://273ventures.com/kl3m-is-first-fairly-trained-llm/.

115. Cory Doctorow, "'Enshittification' Is Coming for Absolutely Everything," *Financial Times*, February 8, 2024, https://www.ft.com/content/6fb1602d-a08b-4a8c-bac0-047b7d64aba5/.

116. Mia Sato, "The Unsettling Scourge of Obituary Spam," *The Verge*, February 12, 2024, https://www.theverge.com/24065145/ai-obituary-spam-generative-clickbait/.

www.ingramcontent.com/pod-product-compliance
Lightning Source LLC
LaVergne TN
LVHW051644050326
832903LV00022B/874